NEW
YORK

**Travel with Marco Polo
Insider Tips**

INSIDER TIP
Your shortcut
to a great
experience

MARCO POLO
TOP HIGHLIGHTS

HIGH LINE ★
A park created on former raised rail tracks in Chelsea – with great views and deckchairs, it's a perfect place to relax.

📷 *Tip: An old billboard at the end of 26th Street gives a great view of the city with the perfect foreground.*

➤ p. 42

9/11 MEMORIAL ★
A total of 2,791 people died in 2001 when the World Trade Center's Twin Towers collapsed. This memorial to the victims of the terror attack is a place for quiet reflection and remembrance right next to one of the world's tallest buildings, One World Trade Center.

➤ p. 32

BROOKLYN BRIDGE ★
It took 13 years to build the "Steel Cathedral" over the East River, but today it takes just 30 minutes to walk across it.

📷 *Tip: To get iconic photos of the skyline, walk from Brooklyn to Manhattan.*

➤ p. 30

STATUE OF LIBERTY ★
This beacon symbolising freedom for both New York and the USA has occupied a prime piece of real estate in New York Harbour since 1886.

📷 *Tip: Some of the best photos of this iconic statue focus on details, such as the crown.*

➤ p. 34

MUSEUM OF MODERN ART
Arguably the world's most import-ant collection of modern art is gathered here. Any artist exhibi-ting at MoMA has truly made it!

➤ p. 50

FIFTH AVENUE 🌟
From the Bergdorf Goodman department store to the Rockefeller Center, this legendary boulevard is lined with luxury shops.
📷 *Tip: Festive lights offer countless photo opportunities in the run-up to Christmas.*

➤ p. 44

CENTRAL PARK 🌟
From bicycle tours to Shakespeare in the Park performances, there is an activity for everyone in New York's green oasis (photo).

➤ p. 51

EMPIRE STATE BUILDING 🌟
The top of this skyscraper offers breathtaking views over Manhattan and out across the landscape beyond.
📷 *Tip: Book a dawn ticket when the light never fails to be amazing.*

➤ p. 44

GUGGENHEIM MUSEUM 🌟
Frank Lloyd Wright's modern masterpiece is one of the best galleries in the city.

➤ p. 54

BROADWAY MUSICALS 🌟
From smash hits like *Hamilton* to older classics like *The Lion King*, Broadway is booming and offers something for everyone

➤ p. 112

CONTENTS

CONTENTS

BEST OF
NEW YORK

A pulsating network of lights illuminates Downtown Manhattan

BEST ☂ WHEN IT RAINS

ACTIVITIES TO BRIGHTEN YOUR DAY

TRAVEL THROUGH MILLENNIA OF ART HISTORY

Egyptian temples, American paintings, fabulous fashion and much, much more. The *Metropolitan Museum of Art*'s collection is unique – you could browse for weeks without getting bored!

➤ p. 52

FLAT WHITE WITH A VIEW

Have a coffee at *Amy's Bread* and watch the vibrant and cosmopolitan streetlife of Hell's Kitchen through the window.

➤ p. 72

BROWSE 10 MILES OF BOOKS

A paradise for bibliophiles, with everything from bestsellers and kids' books to rare art books, the *Strand Book Store* also runs cool events.

➤ p. 91

FEAST IN A FACTORY

Oreos used to be made in the *Chelsea Market* building (photo). They are still on sale today alongside more artisan cakes and everything else, from tacos to lobster.

➤ p. 91

JAZZ & JUICE

Marjorie Eliot holds *"Parlor Entertainment"* jazz concerts in her living room every week. In between the songs, she tells anecdotes or brings glasses of juice around. An amazing experience for a (wet) afternoon.

➤ p. 119

RIVERSIDE EXERCISE

Into bowling, dancing, basketball, climbing, swimming or golf? The range of sports on offer at the huge *Chelsea Piers Sports Center* on the Hudson River is incredible.

➤ p. 126

BEST 🐷
ON A BUDGET

FOR SMALLER WALLETS

MORE THAN JUST A FERRY
The *Staten Island Ferry* (photo) brings commuters into Manhattan for free. Join them for amazing views of the city's skyline and the Statue of Liberty.
➤ p. 34

ART TREASURES ON A BUDGET
Admission to the *Guggenheim* usually costs a punchy $25, but on Saturdays between 6pm and 8pm you can get into this shrine to art for free or for a small donation.
➤ p. 54

GOSPEL THAT STRIKES A CHORD
Gospel church services take place on Sundays across Harlem. People dress in their Sunday best and sing music that is guaranteed to give you goose pimples.
➤ p. 62

FIESTA FOOD UNDER THE HIGHWAY
Munch delicious, good-value tacos from the *Birria-Landia* food truck in Queens. Even the *New York Times* raves about these Mexico-inspired bargain bites.
➤ p. 80

MINI STAGE, MAXI MUSIC
The tiny but innovative *Barbès* club in Brooklyn plays everything from jazz to Balkan beats. And it doesn't charge admission.
➤ p. 114

TAKE A TOUR WITH REAL LOCALS
Big Apple Greeters are a group of passionate and engaged New Yorkers who love showing off their hometown – for free! You'll not only get to know the city, you'll make new friends too.
➤ p. 162

BEST
WITH CHILDREN

FUN FOR YOUNG & OLD

SWIM WITH THE FISHES

Carousels normally go round in circles but the *SeaGlass Carousel* is no normal fairground ride. Its pint-sized passengers don't sit astride horses or at the wheel of fire engines, instead they climb into colourful fish that then appear to descend to the depths of the ocean. A unique experience for kids with a spirit of adventure.

➤ p. 34

PARK LIFE

Bryant Park at the heart of Manhattan offers entertainment all year round with a cinema, fairground and events space in summer and an ice rink in winter.

➤ p. 44

FLIGHT TO THE ISLAND

Kids enjoy riding the subway, so just imagine how excited they get on the *Roosevelt Island Tramway*, a cable car suspended above central New York (photo).

➤ p. 50

MUSEUM ADVENTURES

Stand-out exhibits, including a huge, suspended whale and dinosaur skeletons, ensure the *American Museum of Natural History* is a hit with kids. And it's big enough to keep them entertained for hours.

➤ p. 56

THE ART OF BRICKLAYING

The *Lego Store*'s main purpose is to persuade parents to buy building sets for their kids, but you can also spend hours wandering around and admiring the amazing constructions that can be created from little coloured bricks. There are plenty of opportunities for the kids to get involved, from play areas to live demonstrations.

➤ p. 96

BEST ⚑

CLASSIC EXPERIENCES

ONLY IN NEW YORK

REMEMBRANCE & REGENERATION

The moving *9/11 Memorial* is proof, if ever it was needed, that the New York spirit is indomitable. Water falls into two large basins on the site where the Twin Towers once stood.

➤ p. 32

BRIGHT LIGHTS, BIG CROWDS

Nowhere in New York gets as crowded as world-famous *Times Square*. Find a spot to sit in the pedestrianised section and relax while you watch the world go by.

➤ p. 48

BREATHE IN THE FRESH AIR

Central Park (photo) has been extensively restored, and its flowers, rocks and waterfalls are in great shape. Have a picnic admiring the skyline, join a roller disco or go to an open-air concert. With a zoo and a cable car to boot, there truly is something for everyone.

➤ p. 51

DOUGHNUT DELIGHT

Doughnut Plant's creations come in all shapes and can be filled with anything from peanut butter to blueberry jam.

➤ p. 72

SUPERLATIVE STORE

Macy's is one of the world's biggest department stores and a local institution – it sells everything! And over Thanksgiving weekend, the shop organises a huge parade with floats, music and huge balloons.

➤ p. 93

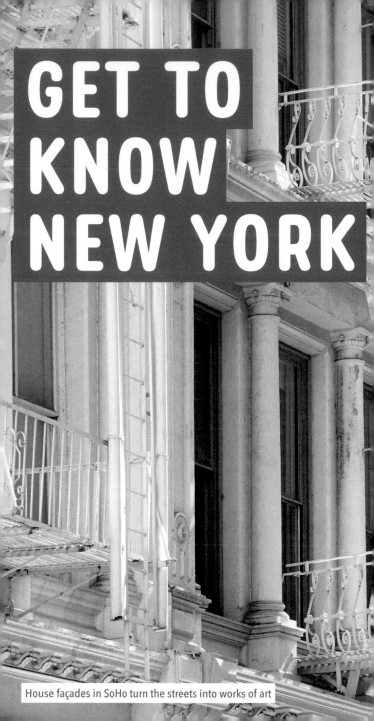

GET TO KNOW NEW YORK

House façades in SoHo turn the streets into works of art

DISCOVER NEW YORK

A special building inside and out: the Guggenheim Museum

New York City is the capital of the American Dream, and the only way to understand this massive, energetic, exciting and globally influential metropolis is to come and see it for yourself. Wake up, alongside 8.5 million New Yorkers, to the sounds of the city that never sleeps – cars hooting, sirens howling and screeching brakes. The New York feeling is simply something you have to experience for yourself.

REGAINED CONFIDENCE AFTER 9/11

New York is big, hectic, loud, provocative and powerful. Since 2015, One World Trade Center (1WTC) has dominated the southern Manhattan skyline at a height

1524
Italian explorer Giovanni da Verrazzano sails into New York's harbour and encounters the indigenous Lenape population

1624
Dutch settlers arrive in the area and call it New Amsterdam

1664
The city is passed over to the British without a fight and becomes New York

1788-1790
New York is the USA's first capital

1886
The Statue of Liberty is installed

1892-1954
More than 12 million people emigrate to New York

of 541m. It symbolises the return of the city's self-confidence after 9/11. Next door to it, the basins of the *9/11 Memorial* mirror the towers that once stood here and the terror attack that brought them down. Just east of the memorial, The Oculus building sits above one of the city's most important subway stations, like an oversized bird in the process of spreading its wings. It is one of the most stunning recent buildings in Manhattan.

CITY OF THE NIGHT

New York is still the world's entertainment capital. Every evening it plays host to classy jazz concerts and cool raves in underground bars while hip hop musicals strut their stuff alongside some of the world's best opera stars. The audiences are varied, enthusiastic and *very* discerning. If you can make it here, you can make it anywhere, as Frank Sinatra sang in his famous hit "New York, New York". In Downtown Manhattan (south of 14th Street), the restaurant and bar scene is more exciting than in Midtown or in northern Manhattan. Trendy new hotels, cool nightclubs and daring architecture – such as the Cooper Union building, the *New Museum of Contemporary Art* and the Frank Gehry Tower (officially 8 Spruce Street) – draw locals and tourists alike to the south of the city. Here run-down buildings sit next to stylish bars, as old mixes with new – a contrast that gives the area its allure. Every year in May the TriBeCa Festival (co-founded by Robert de Niro) takes place. The event is a magnet for movie buffs, celebrity hunters and everyone who is a fan of the glamour of the red carpet.

1952
New York becomes the headquarters for the United Nations (UN)

11 September 2001
Almost 3,000 people are killed in a terror attack on the World Trade Center

2020
The Edge viewing platform is opened in Hudson Yards – it is the world's highest outdoor observation deck

2021
The Coronavirus pandemic claims the lives of 40,000 people in New York

2022
Museum of Broadway opens

CREATIVITY & CONTEMPLATION

As the media capital of the United States, New York hosts major television broadcasters, international magazine companies and the country's biggest newspaper, the *New York Times*. The most important book publishers are also based here. In general, the very best of the creative industries congregate in the city – the glittering concrete jungle, with all its ambition and opportunities, still exerts a powerful pull. However, New Yorkers themselves have become more contemplative. The protest movements Occupy Wall Street and Black Lives Matter, not to mention Donald Trump's election to the White House, shook New York's comfortable sense of America's place in the world. More recently, the Coronavirus pandemic had a particularly profound effect on the metropolis. More than 40,000 New Yorkers died as a result of the virus; shops and restaurants were boarded up, and people left the city. The after-effects will probably be felt for a long time to come; among other things, it is likely that advance reservations will be required for many museums and other attractions for the foreseeable future.

A PLACE FOR POLITICS AWAY FROM D.C.

After World War II, the United Nations set up its headquarters in New York. To this day, its building on the East River is in the spotlight whenever there are discussions over international crises and conflicts, such as the war in Ukraine. New York has also been at the forefront of American politics for years, and this focus intensified following 9/11. But the city is not defined by politics in the same way as Washington D.C. Once the biggest city in the world, New York now has a population of around 8.5 million people and has long since been overtaken in size by other global megacities. That said, 24 million people currently live in the greater metropolitan area, and they are joined by hordes of annual tourists, who are quickly subsumed into the fast-paced urban bustle.

GREEN SHOOTS

Former mayor Michael Bloomberg spearheaded a drive to turn New York into an environmentally friendly city. His efforts are in evidence in Times Square, which is now partially pedestrianised, and in the more than 1,600km of cycle lanes now in place around the city. His successors, Bill de Blasio and Eric Adams, continued to push the green revolution forward on the traffic-heavy streets of Manhattan. In 2017, for example, the Second Avenue Subway was opened, a plan first formulated in 1920; there are currently only three stations on the Upper East Side, but more should be added soon. Traffic islands have been turned into little oases, while a former raised railway track was transformed into the High Line park. The length of Manhattan Island along the Hudson River is now parkland, and much of the riverbank beneath Brooklyn Bridge is now a public space – complete with urban beach, boat trips and playgrounds. New bus lanes forge a green route through the congested streets and environmentally

9/11 Memorial: a poignant memorial to a terribly tragedy

friendly bicycle rickshaws jostle for position. And you can hop on a bike yourself: blue Citi Bikes can be found on nearly every street corner and can be rented in minutes using an app and a credit card.

WALK THE CITY

New York is still a city best explored on foot; indeed, it is perhaps America's only truly pedestrian-friendly city. The grid layout and numerical street numbers are easy to follow; the pavements are wide and many of the city's attractions are located in close proximity to one another. You'll quickly get your bearings, and you'll realise that the risk of street crime is nowadays no higher here than in any other major city. What's more, New York is a city of contrasts. Winters are dry and freezing. The summers are hot (often above 30°C) and very humid. The endless grey concrete jungle juxtaposes with the expansive green of Central Park. Church spires – the tallest buildings in other places – are dwarfed by skyscrapers. And the Big Apple is still a city of immigrants. Almost 40 per cent of its population are first generation Americans. On the whole, immigration is welcomed; many New York immigrants are highly educated (half of the city's doctors were born elsewhere) and ambitious – and, of course, they bring elements of their "home" culture with them. New York is a true melting pot of global traditions, from Ethiopian food culture and Haitian voodoo practices to Italian festivals and Chinese New Year celebrations. The city is a daily social experiment into how different cultures can live together. This multiculturalism has its roots in the city's past as a port, and its success is evident in nearly all aspects of New York life today.

NEW IMMIGRANTS FROM ACROSS THE WORLD

New York's cultural mix is constantly in flux. In the 19th century, immigrants from Ireland, Germany, Austria and Russia sailed up the Hudson River. In the first half of the 20th century, Italian and Polish immigrants joined them. In later decades, the waves of immigration shifted to include people from central and South America, China, Korea and Vietnam, as well as internal migrants from the southern states of the USA. The relative ease with which they have been able to merge, mix and integrate is unique in the United States. It is for this reason that New Yorkers consider themselves as somewhat distinct from the rest of the country, culturally aware, enquiring, tolerant – if occasionally arrogant. In 1989, the first African American mayor of New York, David Dinkins, said, "New York is not a melting pot anymore. It is a gorgeous mosaic of people." Today, sadly there are cracks in this mosaic. At one end of the scale are the newest immigrants, many of whom are poor and may have arrived into the country illegally; at the other end, the salaries in Wall Street are reaching dizzying heights once again – fuelling the ever-rising cost of living. Nonetheless, and perhaps surprisingly, New Yorkers have retained both their sense of humour and their down-to-earth pragmatism.

ONE CITY, FIVE BOROUGHS

Each of the city's five boroughs could be an entire city. Indeed this was the case up until 1898, when Greater New York was formed by merging Manhattan, Brooklyn, Queens, Staten Island and the Bronx. Today, Brooklyn is booming thanks to its museums, architecture, boutiques, sophisticated restaurants and the huge Prospect Park. Williamsburg in northern Brooklyn has become the perfect area for a night out on the town. Young artists and designers here have created a network of galleries, restaurants and interesting small shops. This creative buzz is now spreading east into Bushwick. And slowly but surely the most diverse borough, Queen's, is being discovered by locals and tourists alike thanks to the rapidly growing Long Island City and its surfer beach. But visitors usually stick to the long, thin island of Manhattan – between the Statue of Liberty and Harlem. After all, it is the heart of the city!

AT A GLANCE

8,700,000
population

London: 8,800,000

65,000,000

Tourists per year

837km
Length of coastline

Length of the London stretch
of the Thames: 128km

783.8km^2
surface area

Greater London: 1,572km^2

TALLEST BUILDING ONE WORLD TRADE CENTER

541m

Viewing decks on floors
101–105

CLEAN AIR

23,000

TREES IN CENTRAL PARK

1.68–1.79m

Required height for Radio City Hall's famous dancers, the Rockettes

9,525kg

Weight of the blue whale that hangs
from the ceiling in the American
Museum of Natural History

UP TO 800 LANGUAGES
are estimated to be
spoken in the city

**600,000 DOGS LIVE
IN NEW YORK**

UNDERSTAND NEW YORK

UPTOWN VS DOWNTOWN

Downtown is the southern half of Manhattan and is synonymous with young, up-and-coming and creative New Yorkers, some of whom claim they would never be seen dead north of 14th Street. North of this is Midtown. Central Park starts at 59th Street and with it you hit Uptown. This is where the city's conservative elite lives opulently in apartments with libraries, servants' quarters, huge dining rooms, high ceilings and fireplaces. If you're looking for the creative, hip in-crowd, head south to TriBeCa or the East and West Villages, where the nightlife is innovative and animated.

DESIRABLE DOORMEN

Doormen are status symbols in wealthy areas like the Upper East Side and Upper West Side. There are around 100,000 of them in New York. In apartment blocks where residents have spacious, luxury homes spread over several floors, doormen assist residents by holding open doors, greeting guests, carrying heavy shopping, signing for packages or simply calling a cab. Being a doorman is a well-paid and sought-after job.

ORGANICALLY GREEN

New Yorkers love their farmers' markets where they stock up on sourdough bread and organic fruit and veg. Vendors come from far and wide to sell at one of the more than 60 markets held across the city (full list at *grownyc.org*). Alongside them, organic supermarkets, such as *Trader Joe's* and *Whole Foods*, have huge ranges of perfectly presented organic produce filling their stores. Even the city streets are going green, thanks to the creation of new pedestrian areas and bike paths. With the Citi Bike app on your smartphone and a picnic in your basket, you can visit the city's 1,700 public parks, or take a stroll along the *High Line* in Chelsea – a green space created from old railway tracks that now blooms with wildflowers.

DIZZYING HEIGHTS

If you suffer from vertigo, New York is a good place to overcome it: the city's skyscrapers are some of the tallest in the world. *One World Trade Center* which at 541m is not only the tallest building in the city but in the western hemisphere, was constructed as a replacement for the World Trade Center's Twin Towers, which were destroyed on 11 September 2001 when terrorists flew two hijacked passenger planes into the buildings. Its very existence symbolises that terrorism will not triumph over freedom. When they were completed in 1971 and 1973, the twin towers were themselves part of the city's record-breaking tradition at a height of 419.7m.

The first skyscrapers were built in the late 19th century. The *Chrysler Building* (1930, 319m) and the *Empire State Building* (1931, 443m to the tip of the lightning rod) were just

Farmers' markets bring food fresh from the field into the city

two stand-out examples during a period of monumental construction. Constructing tall buildings was not only down to a shortage of land – it was also a sign of a city growing in confidence, power and also self-consciousness. The art-deco style, brilliantly executed in the Chrysler Building, gave way to the modernism of Ludwig Mies van der Rohe (*Lever House* and *Seagram Building*). Glass, simplicity and functional quality replaced the adornments of the past.

The city's new buildings are no more modest than their predecessors. The grand *8 Spruce Street* – an apartment block with 76 floors by Frank Gehry – opened in 2011 with a rippling façade that appears to move. But it soon ceded its title as the highest residential building in the city to *One57* in Midtown (306m) and just a few months later to *432 Park Avenue*. Opened in 2015, this apartment building tops out at a height of 396m but was itself surpassed by the *Central Park Tower* in 2020 (472m). A new high-rise area is also being developed on the west side of Manhattan near Hudson Yards. Its viewing platform, *Edge (edgenyc.com)*, currently holds the crown for the highest outdoor deck in the world (345m).

ISLAND HOPPING

New York City is made up of a series of islands – a fact that is easy to forget. *Manhattan* itself is one, the Statue of Liberty stands on *Liberty Island*, and *Ellis Island* is where immigrants were received until 1954. A ferry will take you from the southernmost tip of

Manhattan across to *Governors Island* for a picnic on its lawns, on which crazy golf, hammocks and tree houses, art exhibitions and concerts provide entertainment. Kayakers often paddle alongside the ferry to *Staten Island*, one of New York's "Five Boroughs", and you will see hundreds of people getting on or off the blue-and-white ferries at the Brooklyn, Queens and Manhattan docks to go shopping or to get to work. Swinging high over the east end of 60th Street is the aerial tramway that takes you to *Roosevelt Island* in East River.

INSIDER TIP
Two sides to New York

Make sure to walk to the southern tip of Roosevelt Island. On the right is Manhattan and, on the left, Brooklyn – an incredible view! *Randall*

Island can be reached on foot via the bridge on 103rd Street, and the subway and bus will take you to *City Island*, a popular sailing destination. The newly renovated *Coney Island*, a seaside peninsula south of Brooklyn, is once again attracting many visitors, thanks to its amusement parks, rollercoasters, beach, aquarium and tasty food. People from around the world come here to enjoy a stroll along the wide promenade and to enjoy New York island life.

THE COOL NORTH

Harlem is full of energy. Its music, art and restaurant scenes are magnets for people from across the city. And its history is fascinating too. At the beginning of the 20th century, African

Nostalgic and pretty eccentric: Coney Island's Luna Park

Americans from the southern states migrated north to New York. Among them were artists, including the writer Langston Hughes and the subsequently world-famous musicians Duke Ellington and Louis Armstrong. This cultural legacy can still be felt in Harlem and the Bronx, the birthplace of hip hop in the 1970s. *Harlem Heritage Tours (harlemheritage.com)* offer great walking and bus tours, while *Hush Tours (hushtours.com)* explore the city's hip hop heritage. For more on hip hop, visit the dedicated museum at *Bronx Point (uhhm.org)*.

THE WORLD'S A STAGE!

Musicals have always been closely associated with New York, but recent years have seen a resurgence in their popularity, partly thanks to the hype surrounding Lin-Manuel Miranda's hit musical *Hamilton*. Every year, 13 million people come to watch Broadway shows, including such hits as *The Book of Mormon* and *The Lion King*.

If the ticket prices are too high, check out an "Off Off Broadway" show; these are often more interesting and innovative as well as being cheaper. Incidentally, a theatre's proximity to the famous avenue has absolutely nothing to do with it being classed Broadway, Off-Broadway or Off-Off-Broadway. It is all to do with size: Broadway theatres have 500-plus seats; Off-Broadway have 100 to 499 seats and Off-Off-Broadway auditoria have between 50 and 99 seats.

TRUE OR FALSE?

NEW YORK IS DANGEROUS

False! Certainly, until well into the 1990s, New York was famous for its high crime rates: in 1990 more than 2,200 people were killed in the city. But today? New York is no more dangerous than any other big city. You can take the subway at all times of the day, and places once seen as "no-go areas" are now hip, sought-after neighbourhoods – an upside of gentrification, perhaps.

NEW YORK IS A SEASIDE DESTINATION

True! New York is famous for its huge skyscrapers and packed streets so it's easy to forget that the city sits on the sea. A trip out to Coney Island, Brighton Beach, Staten Island, the Bronx Riviera or the Rockaways should be on every itinerary. Take a book or a surfboard and tuck into fish tacos just a few miles from Manhattan's concrete jungle. The city even provides free sun cream!

BARS IN THE CLOUDS

Head to the roof terrace of a Manhattan hotel for sweeping views of the skyscrapers, streetlife and city lights while you drink your cocktail. For the most impressive views, try the *Salon de Ning* at the Peninsula Hotel, *Press Lounge* at Ink48, *Le Bain* at The Standard Hotel, *230 Fifth* on Fifth Avenue or the restaurant atop the Pod39 hotel.

SUMMER ESCAPES

In the summer months it is hot and humid in the city, and many New Yorkers migrate to the countryside. East of the metropolis, there are 100km of fine sand beaches on Long Island, location of the legendary Hamptons, with Fire Island just off-shore. This coastline was once the domain of whalers and smugglers, but it's now where the East Coast in-crowd and Hollywood big names spend their summers feasting on lobster and scallops.

Long Island is in the shape of a crocodile with its mouth open. The *Hamptons* are located along its lower "jaw". These picture-perfect old villages lie along the coast like a string of pearls: South Hampton, Bridge-hampton, East Hampton and Amagansett. Montauk, with its light-house, forms the easternmost point. Charming whitewashed clapboard and wooden houses, narrow streets, small shops and cafés all lend charac-ter to this exclusive and very pricey area.

The thin *Fire Island* is located off Long Island's southernmost point. A boat will take you across. There are no cars, and bicycles are restricted, so you have to carry daypacks for your food, towels and reading material. Wooden walkways lead to the beach. With conservation high on the agenda, the island is full of deer and perfect for birdwatching.

The beaches of *New Jersey* are a cheaper destination. A train from Penn Station takes 1½ hours to Asbury Park where you can swim and surf.

PRICEY PARTS OF TOWN

New York's residents are often on the run, not from the IRS or the law, but from change in their city. Obviously, change is not always bad, but in some areas – such as the housing market – it has broadly been seen as negative. In the 1960s, '70s, and '80s there were still huge swathes of the city where apartments or artists' studios were cheap. Today, the city's rents are among the highest in the world. A one-bed apartment in Manhattan now costs an average of about $3,500 per month. At the same time, around half of the city lives below the poverty line and there is simply not enough hous-ing for them.

The city has got much cleaner and safer in the last few decades. But prices have risen to match. Quaint *Greenwich Village* and buzzing *SoHo* used to be home to lots of authors and artists, but few of them could afford to live there now.

The *Lower East Side* has historically always been a working-class neigh-bourhood where immigrants settled to start their American dream. Some

Williamsburg: no longer an undiscovered idyll in the city

still live there, but gentrification has changed this area too, with posh bars, cafés and galleries taking over from traditional businesses.

Brooklyn was once an oasis of affordability, but its prices now compete with Manhattan. Young creative people have been forced deeper into the borough or out to Queens, the Bronx and Staten Island. As their populations change, these areas develop into cool new cultural centres. For lots of people, the nightlife in Manhattan is too boring, so they head east to Williamsburg and Bushwick in Brooklyn – famous for their music scenes – to party and dance the night away.

SIGHT SEEING

The Empire State Building, SoHo, the Staten Island Ferry, Central Park and Broadway – the constant hustle and bustle of a city that never sleeps can all get a bit overwhelming. So what should you do first, and what are the absolute must-sees?

New York City packs its famously bold architecture into a restricted space: imposing skyscrapers, expansive bridges, stately churches and, in the middle of it all, a park that is the size of a decent-sized town in itself. On top of this, there are excellent museums, incredible views and diverse neighbourhoods.

You'll find all the venues in this chapter on the pull-out map

Autumn brings a colourful glow to Central Park

There is probably no better place in the world to people-watch! Worried that you'll miss something? Relax – there's so much going on in New York that you can guarantee that, wherever you are, you will discover something cool and unique. Walking is the best way to get around the city, but if your feet need a rest, you can always take the subway, hire a bike, hop in a taxi or board a ferry to your destination. The most expensive and exciting way to see the city is from a helicopter. No matter how you travel around, you'll find this is a place with something for everyone. Welcome to New York!

REGIONAL OVERVIEW

MARCO POLO HIGHLIGHTS

★ **BROOKLYN BRIDGE**
Admire the skyline while crossing the "eighth wonder of the world" ➤ p. 30

★ **ONE WORLD TRADE CENTER**
An impressive replacement for the Twin Towers ➤ p. 32

★ **9/11 MEMORIAL**
A poignant memorial ➤ p. 32

★ **STATUE OF LIBERTY**
The city's most symbolic landmark ➤ p. 34

★ **STATEN ISLAND FERRY**
An amazing view of the Manhattan skyline – for free ➤ p. 34

★ **HIGH LINE**
A patch of reclaimed paradise above the streets ➤ p. 41

★ **EMPIRE STATE BUILDING**
Worth the wait: incredible views from the 86th floor ➤ p. 43

★ **FIFTH AVENUE**
Fancy shops to browse and buy in ➤ p. 44

★ **ROCKEFELLER CENTER**
A city within the city ➤ p. 47

★ **MUSEUM OF MODERN ART**
The world's best art gallery ➤ p. 49

★ **CENTRAL PARK**
A green oasis in the city ➤ p. 51

★ **GUGGENHEIM MUSEUM**
Painting and sculpture in a beautiful spiral ➤ p. 54

★ **AMERICAN MUSEUM OF NATURAL HISTORY**
Giant dinosaurs and other earthly delights ➤ p. 56

95
19
Secaucus
Union Ci
95
495
NEW JERSEY
19
John F. Kennedy Boulevard
Hoboken
78
Statue of Liberty

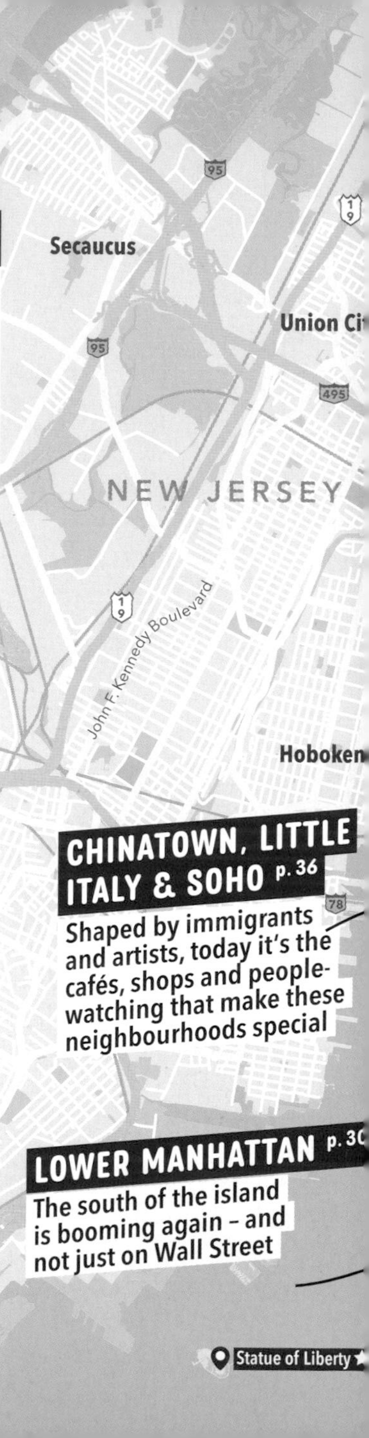

CHINATOWN, LITTLE ITALY & SOHO p. 36

Shaped by immigrants and artists, today it's the cafés, shops and people-watching that make these neighbourhoods special

LOWER MANHATTAN p. 30

The south of the island is booming again – and not just on Wall Street

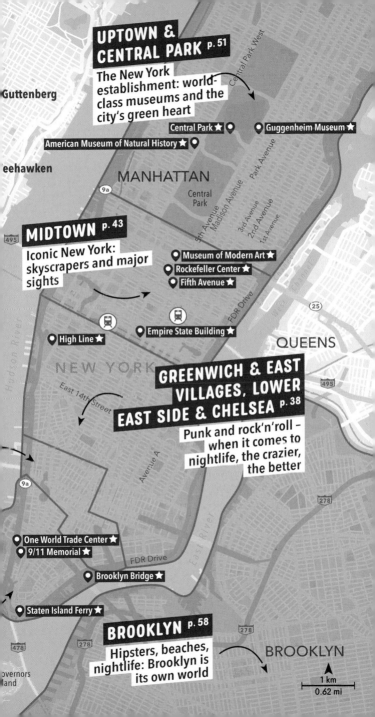

Guttenberg

eehawken

UPTOWN & CENTRAL PARK p. 51

The New York establishment: world-class museums and the city's green heart

Central Park ★ ◉   ◉ Guggenheim Museum ★

American Museum of Natural History ★ ◉

MANHATTAN

Central Park

MIDTOWN p. 43

Iconic New York: skyscrapers and major sights

◉ Museum of Modern Art ★
◉ Rockefeller Center ★
◉ Fifth Avenue ★

◉ Empire State Building ★

◉ High Line ★

QUEENS

NEW YORK

GREENWICH & EAST VILLAGES, LOWER EAST SIDE & CHELSEA p. 38

Punk and rock'n'roll – when it comes to nightlife, the crazier, the better

East 14th Street

Avenue A

◉ One World Trade Center ★
◉ 9/11 Memorial ★

FDR Drive

◉ Brooklyn Bridge ★

◉ Staten Island Ferry ★

BROOKLYN p. 58

Hipsters, beaches, nightlife: Brooklyn is its own world

BROOKLYN

1 km
0.62 mi

overnors
land

LOWER MANHATTAN

Lower Manhattan has it all, from stylish restaurants to historical sites and impressive skyscrapers.

It is home to New York's (and the USA's) financial centre – Wall Street. This is also where the twin towers of the Word Trade Center stood before 9/11; today, One World Trade Center soars above the site of the 9/11 Memorial. Furthermore, this is where, up until the middle of the last century, immigrants arrived to seek their fortune in the "new world". Take a long walk around the gigantic buildings and along the narrow, cobbled streets at the southernmost tip of Manhattan. Don't miss a trip on the ferry to Staten Island – the view of Manhattan's skyline from the water is sensational. Or walk along the Hudson River from Battery Park towards TriBeCa, where the pricey restaurants are very popular with celebrities.

WHERE TO START?

The **Empire State Building** (⌂ E9): The eye-catching art deco skyscraper is the perfect launching pad. Whizz up to the top and enjoy the sweeping views of the city. Fifth Avenue heads north to the major museums and Central Park, and in the south Broadway is only a block away. Watching the sun set here is an unforgettable experience. *Subway: 34 Street-Herald Square, B, D, F, M, N, Q, R*

1 BROOKLYN BRIDGE ★

The first bridge to connect Manhattan with Brooklyn was completed in 1883 after 13 years of construction by engineers John A. Roebling and son. Its two pylons, standing nearly 89m high, support hundreds of steel cables. The structure spans just over 530m above the East River and was once lauded as the "eighth wonder of the world". For the best experience, start in Brooklyn and walk towards the Manhattan skyline. To do so, take subway line A or C to High Street Station in Brooklyn. Alternatively, set out from Manhattan starting from Park Row/Centre Street *(Subway 4,5,6 Brooklyn Bridge/City Hall). ⌂ D17*

> INSIDER TIP
> **Manhattan I'm coming**

2 CITY HALL

Originally, only the southern façade of the mayor's office (completed in 1812) was covered in marble and cheaper brick was used for the northern façade because the city's elders assumed the city would not grow further to the north. Today the building seems oddly incongruous in this huge metropolis, but it is very pretty nonetheless. If you want to tie the knot, go the corner to the *Office of the City Clerk (Mon–Fri 8.30am–3.45pm | 141 Worth Street | register in advance at short. travel/new30).* For $35 dollars you can get a marriage licence which can be used up to 24 hours later. *Broadway/ corner of Park Row Street | Subway 4, 5, 6, Brooklyn Bridge/City Hall | ⌂ B16*

LOWER MANHATTAN

One World Trade Center ★
3 TriBeCa
Brookfield Place **4** **5**
9/11 Memorial ★ **6** **7**
The Oculus
The Skyscraper Museum
Museum of Jewish Heritage **10** **11**
Wall Street **9**
Battery Park **12** **13**
National Museum of the American Indian
16 Staten Island Ferry ★
15 Ellis Island
2 City Hall
8 St Paul's Chapel
Brooklyn Bridge ★
17 South Street Seaport **1**
14 Statue of Liberty ★
Governors Island
750 m
820 yd

3 TRIBECA

The triangle south of Canal Street (*Tri*angle *Be*low *Ca*nal) is the area around the city's former Washington market. Today its renovated warehouses have become stylish residential lofts for the rich and famous. A great place for a wander and a bit of celeb-spotting! *Subway 1 Franklin Street | ⊞ B–C 14–15*

4 BROOKFIELD PLACE

Located west of the World Trade Center, Brookfield Place was formerly the World Financial Center. Now it's an urban centre with offices, shops, flats,

INSIDER TIP
Always something going on

a marina and green spaces. In the Winter Garden – a hall with a glass roof – you'll find numerous restaurants and boutiques, alongside free concerts, exhibitions and displays. *Mon–Sat 10am–8pm, Sun 12–6pm | 230 Vesey Street | bfplny.com | Subway A, C, J, Z, 1, 2, 3 Chambers Street | ⏱ 2 hrs | 🗺 A16*

5 ONE WORLD TRADE CENTER ★

This skyscraper (541m) replaced the Twin Towers, which were destroyed in 2001, and points like an arrow into the sky. There is a visitor centre between floors 100 and 102 with amazing views of New York and, on a clear day, out to Connecticut and New Jersey. The 47-second elevator ride up the western hemisphere's tallest building is an adventure itself, as the glass walls of the lift show the development of Manhattan through the ages – 500 years flash by in no time at all. *Daily 9am–9pm | 117 West Street | admission $43 | oneworldobservatory. com | Subway 1 WTC Cortlandt | ⏱ 1½ hrs | 🗺 A16*

6 9/11 MEMORIAL ★ ⚑

On 11 September 2001, the World Trade Center was razed to the ground when two hijacked passenger aircraft crashed into the twin towers, which had stood on the site since 1973. Ground Zero is now the location of an impressive monument to the terrorist attack: water falls on all sides into deep pools around whose edges the names of all the victims are engraved. This has become a place for memorial and contemplation even as the streets around it have come back to life. *Daily 10am–8pm | 180 Greenwich Street | free admission | 911memorial.com | Subway 1 WTC Cortlandt*

Next to the memorial is an informative and equally moving *Museum (Wed–Mon 10am–5pm | admission $26)*. Firemen, survivors, relatives of the victims and residents give powerful tours of the site. *🗺 A16*

7 THE OCULUS

The area around the 9/11 Memorial has seen a great deal of renovation and new development over the last two decades. The most spectacular

The might of money: Wall Street

example of this is the Oculus. In reality it is just a subway interchange, but it represents so much more. Designed by the Spanish architect Santiago Calatrava, the building looks like a huge white eagle approaching the ground. As well as providing access to numerous subway lines and a regional rail service to New Jersey, the Oculus houses a large shopping mall. It is also a perfect selfie spot! *185 Greenwich Street | Subway 1 WTC Cortlandt | ◫ B16*

8 ST PAUL'S CHAPEL

This small chapel has been a beacon of hope since 1776, notably for sailors far from home and for George Washington, who prayed here on the day of his inauguration in 1789. It remained completely unscathed by the events of 9/11 despite its proximity to the World Trade Center. An exhibition of photos and personal items movingly documents the work of the church after the attack. *209 Broadway/between Vesey and Fulton Street | trinitywallstreet.org | Subway A, C, 1, 2, 3, 4, 5 Broadway Nassau/Fulton Street | ◫ B16*

9 WALL STREET

This small street at Manhattan's southern tip may not be quite as famous if the global economy had not crashed here in 1929. In autumn 1929, the *New York Stock Exchange* become a symbol of both might and misery as thousands of speculators lost their investments, leading to the Great Depression. Wall Street banks were also at the centre of the 2008 financial

crisis and subsequent global recession, which saw the rise of protest movements such as Occupy Wall Street. The Financial District is now booming again, but criticism of its practices and consequent wealth inequalities remains vociferous.

The neo-classical Stock Exchange's visitor gallery has been closed for security reasons since 2001. But don't miss the opportunity for a selfie with either the famous "Charging Bull" statue at the end of Broadway and/or the newer "Fearless Girl" statue opposite the Stock Exchange. *Subway 2, 3, 4, 5 Wall Street | ◫ B17*

10 MUSEUM OF JEWISH HERITAGE

"A living memorial to the Holocaust": this star-shaped museum is a tribute and memorial to the six million Jews who lost their lives at the hands of the Nazis. The exhibits include items from everyday life and from the concentration camps as well as video clips. *Sun, Wed, Thu 10am–5pm, Fri noon-5pm | 36 Battery Place | admission $18, or by voluntary donation after 4pm on Thu | mjhnyc.org | subway 1 South Ferry, 4, 5 Bowling Green | ⊙ 2 hrs | ◫ A17*

11 THE SKYSCRAPER MUSEUM

Find about the history of Manhattan's tallest buildings! A small museum which counts the last remaining architectural model of the World Trade Center among its holdings. Its heavily polished steel floors and ceilings frame the models and create a sense of great height. *Thu–Sat noon–6pm | 39 Battery Place | admission free, book*

LOWER MANHATTAN

tickets online in advance | skyscraper. org | Subway R, 1 Rector Street, 4, 5 Bowling Green | ◷ 1 hr | ▥ A17

⓬ BATTERY PARK

The ferries to Ellis Island and the Statue of Liberty set off from Battery Park. There is an old fort here, several memorials, food trucks and plenty of green space. In fact, from here you can walk all the way up the west side of the island through parkland. Let kids have a go on the 💬 *SeaGlass Carousel (daily 11am–9pm | $5.50 | seaglass carousel.nyc)*, a colourful maritime version of the classic fairground ride, with ride-on fishes transporting children through a fantastical underwater world. *Subway 1 South Ferry 4, 5 Bowling Green | ◷ 2 hrs | ▥ A18*

⓭ NATIONAL MUSEUM OF THE AMERICAN INDIAN 🐃

The old New York Customs Building houses a museum about America's indigenous communities. Its collection is that of the late banker George Gustav Heye and is made up of everyday items like equine jewellery, tents, clothing, etc. It also hosts changing exhibitions showcasing young artists, and it is completely free. *Daily 10am–5pm, Thu until 8pm | 1 Bowling Green | admission free | nmai.si.edu | Subway 1 South Ferry, 4, 5 Bowling Green | ◷ 2–3 hrs | ▥ A18*

⓮ STATUE OF LIBERTY ⭐

Since 1886 "Lady Liberty" has directed her stern gaze towards the east and Europe. Erected by French sculptor Frédéric-Auguste Bartholdi as

a symbol of the political ideals of the United States, the statue stands 46m tall on a 47m-high base and weighs 225 tonnes.

Access to the statue is via the base and a museum that displays the original torch and offers impressive panoramic views over Liberty Island and the skyline.

Ferries to Liberty Island and Ellis Island 9am–4.30pm every 25 mins from the office of the Circle Line, Castle Clinton in Battery Park | factor in waiting time of up to 1 hr for security checks; no large bags allowed | ticket $24 (including admission to the statue base and access to Ellis Island) | statuecruises.com | Subway 1 South Ferry, 4, 5 Bowling Green | ◷ 5–6 hrs (including Ellis Island) | ▥ A21–22

⓯ ELLIS ISLAND

Around 12 million immigrants first stepped onto American soil at this transit centre on a small island in New York Bay between 1892 and 1954. To date, only the main building has been restored, and it houses an interesting museum on migration. To find possible ancestors who made the journey to New York, input your family name online at *heritage.statueofliberty.org/ passenger | info as for the Statue of Liberty above | admission as for Statue of Liberty above (combined ticket) | audio guides available | libertyellis foundation.org | Subway 1 South Ferry, 4, 5 Bowling Green | ▥ A–B19–20*

⓰ STATEN ISLAND FERRY ⭐ 🐃 💬

For the most beautiful view of the Manhattan skyline, take the round trip

The Statue of Liberty is the symbol of the city

on the ferry past the Statue of Liberty and Ellis Island – all for free! When you board, try to nab a spot on the right-hand side of the upper deck. *Daily, every 30 mins (every 15 mins in rush hour) | 4 South Street/Whitehall Street | siferry.com | Subway 1 South Ferry | ⏷ B18*

🔟 SOUTH STREET SEAPORT

This old port area is one of the best-preserved bits of old New York, despite suffering extensive damage in Hurricane Sandy in 2012. Since then, it has had something of a renaissance. Its cobbled streets are filled with cool restaurants and shops, and there is a museum about the area. The mall by the water's edge has amazing views of the skyline and Brooklyn Bridge from its roof. In summer, the events space is turned into a gig venue; in winter, it is a skating rink. *Subway A, C, J, Z, 2, 3, 4, 5 Fulton Street | ⊞ C17–18*

CHINATOWN, LITTLE ITALY & SOHO

New York's diversity is particularly apparent in these districts. The smells, tastes and cultural artefacts of many different countries crowd the senses on these bustling streets. Here you can travel the world without leaving the city.

Chinese food shops, pizzerias, smart boutiques, pricey galleries, Vietnamese restaurants and Italian cafés all invite you to stop, look, sample and get involved. There are now several *Chinatowns* in the city, but this is the original and the best. The first Chinese people came here at the end of the 19th century and settled, gradually buying up property until they began to become the majority community, with shops, restaurants, bakeries and markets. New Yorkers come here from across the city for delicious, good-value food.

The Italian community that settled in *Little Italy* at the beginning of the 20th century is finding it harder to maintain its identity. Chinatown is encroaching across the old Canal Street border. Yuppies are moving into the expensive apartments, and tourists throng the streets. But you can still order a good cappuccino in a café here and drink in some Italian atmosphere.

To the west of Little Italy lies *SoHo*. The name means *So*uth of *Ho*uston Street. This district between Broadway and Avenue of the Americas was discovered by artists at the start of the 1970s. Galleries and boutiques soon followed suit. Today SoHo is New York's best shopping area, if a pricey one.

🔞 CANAL STREET

Canal Street separates the districts of West Village and SoHo from neighbouring TriBeCa. This is also where Little Italy borders Chinatown. The further east you go, the more the Chinese community's influence is felt. It seems as though you can buy anything on this street, although the branded goods tend not to be original or authentic. *Subway A C, E, N, Q, R Canal Street | ⊞ B14–D15*

🔞 MUSEUM OF CHINESE IN AMERICA

If you want to learn more about the Chinese community in America, you need to visit this often-overlooked but worthwhile museum. There is an excellent permanent exhibition as well interesting temporary ones and a fun museum shop.

A couple of streets away the new *Italian American Museum (155 Mulberry Street | italianamerican museum.org, visit the website for*

CHINATOWN, LITTLE ITALY & SOHO

21 Greene Street

22 New Museum of Contemporary Art

20 Broadway

MANHATTAN

19 Museum of Chinese in America

18 Canal Street

Seward Park

400 m
437 yd

up-to-date opening times and admission prices) does a similar job for the local Italian community. *Thu 11am–9pm, Fri-Sun 11am–6pm | 215 Center Street | admissions $12 | mocanyc.org | Subway 4, 5, 6, J, Q, R Canal Street | ⏱ 1–2 hrs | ▢ C15*

20 BROADWAY

Cutting right through the middle of New York, Broadway is not only its most famous street but also its longest. It starts at the southernmost tip of Manhattan and stretches over 13 miles north. Unusually for NYC's grid,

Broadway isn't straight. It makes its way from the East Side straight through Midtown and the Upper West Side and on to Harlem following an old trade path used by the Lenape community. *Subway B, D, F, M Broadway-Lafayette | 🕮 A17*

21 GREENE STREET

SoHo is known for its well-preserved cast-iron buildings and cobbled streets. The historic area is characterised by ornate and decorative 19th-century facades and Greene Street has some of the best examples.

> **INSIDER TIP**
> **Cast-iron sculpture**
>
> You can get into some of them too, including the erstwhile home of the artist Donald Judd

(tours Tue–Sat, book online | admission $27.50 | 101 Spring Street | juddfoundation.org | Subway 6 Spring Street) 🕮 C14

22 NEW MUSEUM OF CONTEMPORARY ART

A pile of outsized shoe boxes? No, a building of great beauty. Thankfully the avant garde art inside matches the cool exterior of Manhattan's most innovative museum. *Tue–Sun 11am–6pm, Thu until 9pm | 79 Essex Street, between Delencey and Broom | admission $18, or by voluntary donation after 7pm on Thu | newmuseum.org | Subway, B, D, F, M Broadway-Lafayette | 🕚 1–2 hrs | 🕮 D14*

GREENWICH & EAST VILLAGES, LOWER EAST SIDE & CHELSEA

Until the 1960s, *Greenwich Village* was the domain of writers, artists and professors from New York University.

Today it has evolved into a low-rise expensive residential area. Many of its "brownstones" and "town houses" still have their magnificent original 19th-century staircases. Quite uncharacteristically for Manhattan, here the narrow streets have names, not numbers. East of Greenwich is *East Village*, popular among young people. The

High-end shopping in SoHo

Authentically Chinese: a shop on Canal Street

old Jewish, Polish and Russian district between Bowery and Avenue A as well as between 1st and 12th Streets used to be a colourful bohemian artists' district. However, rising rents have forced many artists to move out to Brooklyn and Queens. Street chic is still very much in vogue here, and it is an excellent place to eat as there are many reasonably priced restaurants showcasing cuisines from around the globe, meaning you can take a culinary world tour in one evening.

The *Lower East Side* became famous – indeed infamous – as the home of many of the poor European immigrants that arrived in the city at the end of the 19th century. The Tenement Museum documents the appalling living conditions the immigrants endured in their new homeland. Today, the district is fresh, dynamic, exciting and energetic with plenty of galleries, quaint designer shops and unconventional bars.

Chelsea was once where the LGBTQ community came to party. Partially thanks to developments like the High Line, it is today one of the most expensive districts in the city. This has brought a large number of excellent but expensive galleries into the area.

🗺 WASHINGTON SQUARE 🏳️‍🌈

Jugglers, mime artists, hip hop dancers, balloon artists – this is busker central! The square has an eventful past and a colourful present. It contains the Washington Arch – built to commemorate the centenary of the inauguration of the first American president, George Washington. It was once a cemetery and execution site. Today, the southwest side has a small but decent adventure playground that is ideal for family picnics. But it's not only children that enjoy this rare patch of green in Downtown; they share it with street musicians, joggers and students, all of whom revel in its special atmosphere. *Subway A–F, M W 4 Street | ⊞ D13*

INSIDER TIP
Downtown picnic with the kids

24 CHRISTOPHER STREET

In the heart of Greenwich Village lies the hub of New York's *LGBTQ community*. It has pubs, bars and shops, and it serves as a symbol of respect and acceptance. *Subway 1 Christopher Street | ⊞ B–C12*

25 WHITNEY MUSEUM OF AMERICAN ART

This highly acclaimed Renzo Piano building is packed with 20th-century American art, and its light-filled galleries and terraces have amazing views. *Mon, Wed/Thu 10.30am–6pm, Fri 10.30am–10pm, Sat/Sun 11am–6pm | 99 Gansevoort Street | admission $25, Fri after 7pm a voluntary donation | whitney.org | Subway A, C, E L 14th Street | ⊙ 2 hrs | ⊞ B11*

26 LITTLE ISLAND

Media mogul Barry Diller is responsible for bankrolling one of the city's

Chess games on Washington Square – enthusiasts are welcome to take up the challenge

GREENWICH & EAST VILLAGES, LOWER EAST SIDE & CHELSEA

27 High Line ★

26 Little Island

25 Whitney Museum of American Art

28 Rubin Museum of Art

MANHATTAN

24 Christopher Street

23 Washington Square

30 St Marks Place

29 Merchant's House Museum

31 Tenement Museum

32 International Center of Photography

500 m
547 yd

---

newest attractions: a park island on stilts in the Hudson River. It's a spectacular spot for a picnic, day or night. *Daily 6am-midnight, reserve tickets in advance at busy periods | free admission | Park West 13th Street | littleisland.org | Subway A, C, E, L 14 Street | ▥ B11*

27 HIGH LINE ★

The High Line runs directly past the Whitney Museum. It's a park created on old railway tracks. You can saunter north along it for over a mile, taking in great views and admiring beautiful flowers and trees along the way. *thehighline.org | ▥ B–C 9–11*

---

28 RUBIN MUSEUM OF ART 🌂

Paintings from Bhutan, fabrics from China, sculptures from Tibet: this Chelsea museum contains Buddhist art from the Himalayas, some of it centuries old, some of it brand new. Round off your visit with a cocktail, a salad or an Asian snack in the trendy bar. *Thu, Sat, Sun 11am–5pm, Fri 11am–10pm | 150 W 17th Street/ between 6th and 7th Av. | admission $19, free after 6pm on a Fri | rmanyc. org | Subway F, L, M 14th Street | ◷ 1–2 hrs | ▥ D11*

29 MERCHANT'S HOUSE MUSEUM

The home of an affluent ironmonger is the city's only house from the 19th century whose interior is still intact. *Thu–Sun 1–5pm, also Wed June–Aug. Guided tour at noon Thu–Sun. | 29 E 4th Street/between Lafayette Street and Bowery | admission $15 | merchantshouse.com | Subway 6 Astor Place | ◷ 1 hr | ▥ 13*

30 ST MARKS PLACE

It may only be three blocks of 8th Street that get called St Marks Place, but they have always acted as a kind of cool gateway to the East Village. Great people-watching, cool vintage shops and varied restaurants. *Subway F 2nd Av. | ▥ E13*

31 TENEMENT MUSEUM

In the 19th century people came from countries like Poland, Germany, Ireland and Ukraine and helped to build New York. However, their living conditions were grim, with large families packed into tiny tenements. This superb museum tells their fascinating stories on interactive tours of a renovated tenement and through

INSIDER TIP
The people who built Ne York

the streets of the Lower East Side. *Daily 10am–6pm | 103 Orchard Street | admission $30 | tenement.org | Subway A, C, E, F, M, J, Z Delancey Street-Essex Street | ◷ 2–3 hrs | ▥ E15*

32 INTERNATIONAL CENTER OF PHOTOGRAPHY

Videos, art, projects, photojournalism, presentations: the trendy photo museum hosts changing exhibitions of work by well-known and upcoming photographers. There's a pleasant café and a well-stocked shop in the foyer. *Wed–Mon 11am–7pm, Thu until 9pm | admission $16, or by donation on Thu from 6pm | 79 Essex Street, between Delancey and Broome streets | icp.org | Subway F, J, M, Z Delancey Street-Essex Street | ◷ 1–2 hrs | ▥ E15*

Sunbathing on the High Line

MIDTOWN

Midtown is a hectic working district with a permanent buzz on its skyscraper-filled streets.

But thankfully you are not in a rush! Take time to admire the splendours of the art-deco Chrysler Building and the renovated Grand Central Terminal, stylish luxury apartment blocks and some remarkable museums. At night take in a musical on Broadway, or go to a jazz concert or the opera.

33 EDGE

There are spectacular views from the highest outdoor viewing platform in the western hemisphere. Nearby in Hudson Yards, discover The Shed exhibition space and The Vessel artwork. *Daily 8am–midnight | 30 Hudson Yards | admission from $38 | edgenyc. com | Subway 7, 34th Street-Hudson Yards | ⊞ C8*

34 MUSEUM OF SEX

Things get a bit steamy at this Fifth Avenue museum! The Museum of Sex has historical and artistic exhibits, but its main themes are the pleasures of eroticism and the business of sex. *Mon, Wed, Thu 1–10pm, Fri 1pm–midnight, Sat noon–midnight, Sun noon–10pm | admission (over-18s only) from $36 | 233 5th Av./27th Street | museumofsex.com | Subway N, R 28th Street | ⏲ 1–2 hrs | ⊞ E10*

35 EMPIRE STATE BUILDING ★

It is 443m to the very tip of the lightning conductor on top of this 102-storey monolith in granite and steel. Built in just 18 months and opened in 1931, this early skyscraper is one of the most iconic symbols of New York. At night it is lit up (in red, white and blue on 4 July). A super-fast lift will take you up to the freshly renovated viewing deck, where you can see for up to 80km on a clear day.

Visiting at sunset is a particularly memorable experience. *Daily 11am–midnight | 350 5th Av./34th Street | admission from $44 | esbnyc.com | Subway B, D, F, M, N, Q, R 34th Street-Herald Square | ⏲ 1–2 hrs | 🕮 E9*

36 FIFTH AVENUE ★

This is where New York's large parades take place (e.g. on Thanksgiving and Saint Patrick's Day). It is also home to New York's grandest shops (including Tiffany's and the department store Bergdorf Goodman), superb museums (such as the Metropolitan Museum and the Guggenheim) and architectural delights (such as the Rockefeller Center and the Empire State Building).

You will soon notice that Fifth Avenue, which begins in the south on Washington Square and ends at the island's northern tip, serves as an important orientation point in this concrete jungle becausee it marks the dividing line between West (W) and East (E) on Manhattan's numbered streets. *🕮 F8*

An icon among skyscrapers: the Empire State Building

37 BRYANT PARK

The future is finally here: a park with WiFi! If you don't need to use the fast broadband, you can play chess or table tennis, photograph your children on the carousel, or watch an outdoor movie in the evening – all for free! This green gem among the *skyscrapers* is a perfect place for a break – not least because it probably has the cleanest public toilets in the city. *42nd Street between 5th and 6th Av. | bryantpark.org | Subway B, D, F, M 42nd Street-Bryant Pk. | 🕮 F8*

INSIDER TIP
A perfect (loo) stop

38 NEW YORK PUBLIC LIBRARY

This grand library has been used so often in films that it has become something of a poster boy for public libraries. Stone lions called "Patience" and "Fortitude" (as every New York school kid knows) flank the entrance

to the 1911 Beaux Arts building. Its wood panelled reading room (with internet access) holds excellent exhibitions. It houses treasures like a handwritten annotated version of the Declaration of Independence by Thomas Jefferson, a Gutenberg Bible and manuscripts by Galileo Galilei.

There's a great view of the library and Bryant Park from the new roof terrace of the library's annexe, diagonally opposite to the southeast on Fifth Avenue. *Mon, Thu–Sat 10am–6pm, Tue, Wed 10am–8pm, Sun 1–5pm, closed Sat–Mon in summer | free tours available (book in advance) from nypl. org/events/tours/schwarzman | 476 5th Av. | nypl.org | Subway B, D, F, M 42nd Street | ☐ F9*

39 GRAND CENTRAL TERMINAL

Some 88 million cubic feet of soil had to be excavated, 15 miles of railway tracks laid and around 18,000 tons of steel produced to build this massive train station in 1913. More than 150,000 people attended the opening of the Grand Central Terminal over a century ago. Its main concourse's roof is higher than Notre Dame's and its façade is beautifully decorated with Beaux Arts detail. Above its 25m-high windows, 2,500 stars are painted into its vaulted ceiling.

Today the terminal is sadly only served by suburban commuter trains. Restaurants and fast-food joints (in the basement) as well as many shops fill the arcade. From the gallery level, there is a great view. There is a surprise on the lower ground floor.

INSIDER TIP
Whisper sweet nothings

Find a spot by a column in one of the corners near the Oyster Bar. If your partner goes to the other side, you need not share your secrets with anyone else!

The *Municipal Art Society of New York* offers an entertaining tour of Grand Central *(daily 12.30pm | meet at the entrance to track 29/Main Concourse | $30 | tel. 1 212 4 64 82 55 | mas.org/event-type/tour/)*. For a different perspective, you can look down on the station from the viewing platform atop One Vanderbilt, a giant skyscraper that looms nearby *(admission $39 | summitov.com). Access to the* Instagram-worthy mirror installation is included. *89 E 42nd Street | Subway 4–7, S Grand Central | ☐ F9*

40 CHRYSLER BUILDING

A favourite skyscraper among New Yorkers, this magnificent art-deco building dates back to 1930. Even though the top is off limits, a visit to its lobby with its marble floors, murals and 18 lifts – with doors manufactured from a variety of woods – is well worth it. Built by architect William van Alen for the Chrysler motor vehicle group, its elegant and distinctive exterior was a play on the chrome-laden features (like the radiator grills) of the Chrysler cars. *405 Lexington Av./between 42nd and 43rd Street | Subway 4–7, S Grand Central | ☐ G9*

41 UNITED NATIONS

A meeting place for the whole world, this complex of three skyscrapers is the United Nations headquarters. Join a guided tour if you want to stand at the lectern once used by Barack Obama, Tony Blair and the Pope. *Mon–Fri 9.30am–4.45pm | 1st Av./46th Street | admission $22 | visit.un.org | Subway 6 51st Street | ⏱ 1–2 hrs | ☐ H9*

42 MADISON AVENUE

The 1960s was the golden age of the "Mad Men", the "Men of Madison Avenue". And there has rarely been so much smoking, drinking and machismo on display as in the offices portrayed in the hit TV series about

The atmospheric New York Public Library is always worth a visit

them. This view of the world of the New York advertising business, for which Madison Avenue is still famous, is said to have been faithful to reality. Today the avenue is also famous for being one of the most expensive shopping streets in the world. Any luxury brand you can name will have a store here. *E11*

ST PATRICK'S CATHEDRAL

The largest Catholic church in the States has space for 2,500 worshippers. A tranquil spot to seek solace and catch your breath from the hustle and bustle of 5th Avenue at any time of day. The stone and marble neo-Gothic cathedral was dedicated to the Irish patron saint in 1879 and is the seat of New York's Catholic archdiocese. *5th Av./50th Street | Subway B, D, F, M 47th–50th Street | G8*

ROCKEFELLER CENTER ★

In the 1930s, oil tycoon John D. Rockefeller Jr had 228 houses torn down to build this "city within a city". The complex is made up of 14 skyscrapers – among them the 70-storey high *Comcast Building* (formerly the General Electric Building), squares, gardens, the *Radio City Music Hall, Christie's* auction house and the broadcaster NBC. The viewing platform *Top of the Rock (admission $40 | topoftherocknyc.com)* on the 70th floor offers spectacular views across midtown Manhattan and Central Park.

You can also have a drink on the 65th floor at the renowned Rainbow Room where the view is every bit as good. From mid-November the Rockefeller Center is home to one of the city's most beautiful sights: a huge brightly lit Christmas tree and an ice rink are set up in the main plaza. *30 Rockefeller Plaza/between 49th and 50th Street | rockefellercenter.com | Subway B, D, F, M 47th–50th Street | ⏱ 2–3 hrs | 🗺 F7*

45 RADIO CITY MUSIC HALL

This art-deco concert hall in the Rockefeller Center seats 6,000 at capacity and, when it opened in 1932, it was the world's biggest. Today there are concerts of all kinds here, as well as the Rockettes' Christmas show and a house dance troupe. *1260 Av. of the Americas/between 50th and 51st Street | msg.com/radio-city-music-hall | Subway B, D, F, M 47th–50th Street | 🗺 F7*

46 THEATER DISTRICT

This is the place to celebrate New Year. More than one million New Yorkers traditionally gather at ⚑ *Times Square* at midnight listening to music, watching light shows and waiting for the famous *ball drop* – when the Times Square Ball falls to announce the start of the new year. To see it all, you have to get there very early and, to be honest, you can come any night to see the lights, take a photo with a "Disney character", attend a musical or people watch. Before a show visit the new *Museum of Broadway (admission $39 | 145 West 45th Street | themuseumof broadway.com)* and then, after the performance, head to *Restaurant Row*

on 46th Street (between Eighth and Ninth Avenue) for a bite to eat. *Subway N, R, S, 1–3, 7, Q 42nd Street/Times Square | ⊞ E7*

47 MUSEUM OF MODERN ART ★

Many regard the recently renovated and expanded MoMA as the world's best art museum because of it incredible 20th-century collection, which includes masterpieces by the likes of Henri Matisse, Vincent van Gogh, Frida Kahlo and Pablo Picasso. Since 1929 the museum has acquired 200,000 top-quality works of all kinds and it also holds excellent temporary exhibitions. See where your mood takes you and after you have had enough head to the charming sculpture garden or browse in the superb shop. *Sun–Fri 10.30am–5.30pm, Sat 10.30am–7pm | 11 W 53rd Street/ between 5th and 6th Av. | admission $25 | moma.org | Subway B, D, F, M 47th–50th Street | ⏱ 2–3 hrs | ⊞ F7*

48 SONY BUILDING (550 MADISON AVENUE)

This skyscraper, designed by Philip Johnson and clad in pink granite, is a post-modern classic. Take a glance into the lobby to see why it's not just architects who love it. *550 Madison Av./between 55th and 56th Street | Subway N, R 5th Av./59 Street | ⊞ G7*

There are higher viewing decks, but the one at the Rockefeller Center is pretty special

Gaze out at the city through the glass of the luxurious One Columbus Circle

49 TRUMP TOWER

In 1983, long before he was president, property developer Donald Trump built a monument to himself. The penthouse on top of this 200m-high building, with its waterfalls and golden escalators was once his main residence and the foyer is filled with restaurants and stores – the Trump name is everywhere. *725 5th Av./ between 56th and 57th Street | Subway N, R 5th Av./59th Street | ◻ G7*

50 ROOSEVELT ISLAND TRAMWAY 😊

A cable car floats out over East River to Roosevelt Island roughly every 15 minutes. *Sun–Thu 6am–2am, Fri, Sat 6am–3.30am | Entrance: 59th Street and 2nd Av. | Price $ 2,75 (Metrocard) | rioc.ny.gov | Subway N, R, 4–6 Lexington Av./59th Street | ◻ H7*

51 ONE COLUMBUS CIRCLE

The twin towers of One Columbus Circle are 229m high. Inside are a hotel, a shopping mall, jazz venues and nice restaurants. *10 Columbus Circle | the shopsatcolumbuscircle. com | Subway A–D, 1 59th Street-Columbus Circle | ◻ F6*

UPTOWN & CENTRAL PARK

Uptown has always been seen as the home of the affluent and cultured elite of New York society.

To some extent this stereotype no longer holds true, due to the number of successful people who are now moving south into huge trendy lofts in TriBeCa or pretty Greenwich Village. Nevertheless, on the Upper East and Upper West Sides you will find interesting architecture, world-class large museums and plenty of opportunities to observe wealthy New Yorkers at work or at play in gourmet markets or when they take their dogs for the fanciest dog massages you can possibly imagine.

The area between the Hudson and Central Park is called the *Upper West Side*. Columbus Avenue is lined with expensive shops, while Amsterdam Avenue is home to lots of restaurants. On Broadway you will come across traditional delis like *Zabar's*. The Museum of Natural History and the Lincoln Center, housing the Metropolitan Opera, are the cultural attractions here. The *Upper East Side* is traditionally more conservative than its western counterpart. The district between Central Park and East River has to a large extent been upmarket in character since the end of the 19th century. The Metropolitan Museum and the Guggenheim Museum are located here, as are expensive boutiques and several high-end hotels.

52 CENTRAL PARK ★ ⚑

A green giant almost twice the size of the principality of Monaco, the park stretches over 843 acres. After a planning phase that lasted two decades under Frederick Law Olmsted, the park was finally completed in 1873. New Yorkers take full advantage of it, jogging round the lake or rowing on it *(from $20 plus $20 in cash as a security deposit)*; riding bikes, rollerblading and, in winter, ice-skating on the *Wollman Rink (admission $14, Fri–Sun $23, skate hire $11)*; wandering around the *Central Park Zoo (centralparkzoo. com)* or meeting in its cafés and restaurants. In summer, the park stages free concerts – of anything from classical music to rock – and there is an open-air cinema and *Shakespeare in the Park*.

At *Strawberry Fields (W 72nd Street)* near the Dakota building on the western edge of the park, you can pay tribute to murdered Beatle John Lennon. *centralparknyc.com* | *Subway A–D, 1 59 Street-Columbus Circle; B, C 72 Street* | ⌖ *F6–K1*

53 FRICK COLLECTION

Industrialist Henry Clay Frick's exquisite collection of art housed in his Beaux Arts palace will give you an insight into the obsession that rich Americans have with art. There are paintings by Rembrandt, Holbein, Vermeer, Goya and Renoir, as well as historic furniture. After a circuit of the rooms, sit down for a rest by the fountain in the courtyard.

The Frick mansion was closed for renovations in early 2021, with highlights from the collection on show in the brutalist Breuer building at Madison Avenue/75th Street. Check the website for reopening details! *Thu–Sun 10am–6pm | 1 E 70th Street/5th Av. (temporary home at Frick Madison, 945 Madison Av) | admission $22, Thu 4–6pm by voluntary donation | frick.org | Subway 6 68th Street | ⏱ 1–2 hrs | 🗺 H5*

54 METROPOLITAN MUSEUM OF ART ☂

The huge flight of stairs leading up to the imposing façade of the museum (founded 1870) is a popular place for New Yorkers to take a break before or after a visit to the "Met", one of the world's largest museums. There is little to see of the original structure: New York's most prestigious museum has been extended in all directions so that it now encroaches on neighbouring Central Park – despite this expansion, only a quarter of its three million items can be exhibited at one time.

This place can be overwhelming: it is hard to know where to start and what to see. One unmissable area is the Egyptian wing (ground floor on the right) which has the original Temple of Dendur. Masterpieces by Rembrandt, Caravaggio and El Greco can be found on the first floor. You're best off wandering around and seeing what catches your eye, whether its art from Ancient Greece or Rome, from the Middle East or, indeed, the Middle Ages. Perhaps you prefer musical instruments, etchings, guns, prints or maybe photographs. If you're visiting between April and October don't miss the roof terrace. It has spectacular views of the

INSIDER TIP
Cocktail wi[th]
a view

The Metropolitan Museum of Art is one of the world's finest museums

UPTOWN & CENTRAL PARK

NEW JERSEY
Cliffside Park

NEW YORK

66 Columbia University

64 Upper Manhattan

65 Saint John the Divine

MANHATTAN

Wards
Island

Hell
Gate

63 Children's Museum
of Manhattan

57 Museum Mile

Central Park ★ 52

56 Guggenheim Museum ★

American Museum
of Natural History ★ 59

55 Neue Galerie

60 New York
Historical
Society

54 Metropolitan Museum of Art

Central Park West 58

62 61 American Folk Art Museum

Lincoln Center
for the
Performing Arts

53 Frick Collection

1 km
0.62 mi

---

park and the New York skyline ... and a bar. The museum's annual fashion exhibitions are also increasingly popular. *Sun–Tue, Thu 10am–5pm, Fri, Sat until 9pm | 1000 5th Av. | admission $30. Tickets are valid for 3 days and can be used at the Met Cloisters too | metmuseum.org | Subway 4–6 86th Street | ⏱ 3–4 hrs | ⊞ H–J 3–4*

55 NEUE GALERIE NEW YORK

The "New Gallery" houses German and Austrian art, which had an important impact on modern American art, architecture and design. The collection includes work by Gustav Klimt, Egon Schiele, Paul Klee and artists from the "Brücke", "Blauer Reiter" and Bauhaus movements. The Viennese-style coffeeshop, *Café Sabarsky*, serves Austrian specialities as well as hosting occasional *cabaret dinners. Thu–Mon 10am–5pm | 1048 5th Av./86th Street | admission $25 | neuegalerie.org | Subway 4–6 86th Street | ⏱ 2 hrs | ▥ J3*

56 GUGGENHEIM MUSEUM ⭐

The Guggenheim's extraordinary building designed by American master Frank Lloyd Wright is sometimes described as a tea cup or a multistorey car park by its critics. Temporary exhibitions of modern art are on display along its upward spiralling ramp that goes up four floors from street level. A permanent exhibition from the collection of copper magnate Solomon Guggenheim includes works by van Gogh, Monet, Degas and Picasso. *Sun, Mon, Wed–Fri 11am–6pm, Sat 11am–8pm | 1071 5th Av. between 88th and 89th Street | admission $25, or by 🐷 voluntary donation Sat 6–8pm | guggenheim.org | Subway 4–6 86th Street | ⏱ 2–3 hrs | ▥ J3*

57 MUSEUM MILE

You've already ticked off the "Met", the Guggenheim, the Frick Collection and the Neue Galerie, but you're still hungry for more? Never fear, the "Museum Mile" continues north along Fifth Avenue. Discover the design museum *Cooper Hewitt (Wed–Mon 10am–6pm | 2 E 91st Street | Eintritt $18 | cooperhewitt.org | ▥ J3) and The Jewish Museum (Fri–Mon 11am–6pm, Thu 11am–8pm | 1109 5th Av./92nd Street | admission $18 | thejewish museum.org | ▥ J3)*, which has

excellent special exhibitions. Or learn all about the city's history in the *Museum of the City of New York (Fri–Mon 10am–5pm, Thu 10am–9pm | 1220 5th Av./103rd Street | admission $20 | mcny.org | ▥ K1)* and finally, soak up some Hispanic-American culture in *El Museo del Barrio (Thu–Sun 11am–5pm | 1230 5th Av. | admission $9 | elmuseo.org | ▥ K1)*.

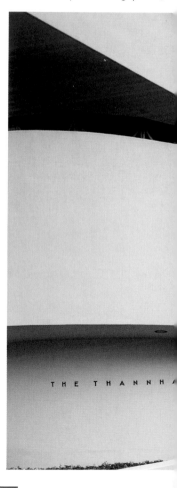

THE THANNH

58 CENTRAL PARK WEST

In the late 19th century, enterprising developers had to come up with ways to lure tenants from Fifth Avenue to the then relatively unattractive west of the city. They built imposing apartment blocks, furnished and decorated in the most lavish style, and provided servants to cater for the new residents' every whim. Among the buildings is the *Dakota* on the north side of 72nd Street – the building where Beatle John Lennon was shot dead by a deranged fan in 1980 – the *Beresford (81st Street)*, the *San Remo (74th/75th Street)* and the *Hotel Des Artistes (1 W 67th Street)*. Unfortunately, you can't get inside, but they are stunning to look at. *Subway B, C 72nd Street |* ⊞ *F–K 1–6*

The Guggenheim Museum's spiral-shaped building is world famous

59 AMERICAN MUSEUM OF NATURAL HISTORY ★ ☺

A huge blue whale, even bigger dinosaur skeletons, gems, meteorites and much more. The AMNH holds around 36 million objects and is not just fun for kids. There is information on the first settlers of the continent, and on the development of organisms, eco-systems and whole universes. *Wed–Sun 10am–5.30pm | Central Park West/79th Street | admission $23 | amnh.org | Subway B, C 81st Street | ⟳ 3–4 hrs | ▥ G3*

60 NEW YORK HISTORICAL SOCIETY

Dating back to 1804, this is the city's oldest museum. Among the displays are photos from 1850 to the present day, and everyday items including newspapers, letters and an impressive collection of glass lamps by Louis Comfort Tiffany. *Tue–Thu, Fri 11am–8pm, Sat, Sun 11am–5pm | 170 Central Park W | admission $22, or by voluntary donation on Fri 6–8pm | nyhistory.org | Subway B, C 81st Street | ⟳ 1–2 hrs | ▥ G4*

61 AMERICAN FOLK ART MUSEUM

A museum full of artisanal work, from saddlecloths made by indigenous Americans to quilts made by settlers, right up to modern crafts. Even better – it is all free and it has a great shop!! *Wed–Sun 11.30am–6pm | 2 Lincoln Square/66th Street | admission free | folkart-museum.org | Subway 1 66th Street | ⟳ 1–2 hrs | ▥ F5*

There are dinosaurs, spaceships and much more in the American Museum of Natural History

62 LINCOLN CENTER FOR THE PERFORMING ARTS

This is the cultural heart of New York. In the 1960s a whole city district was demolished to build the Lincoln Centre. (Before they were pulled down, the empty houses were used as the set for *West Side Story*.) The focal point is the plaza which holds everything from salsa lessons to rock concerts in the summer. In the surrounding buildings, there is space devoted to jazz and classical music, ballet and cinema – and all of it is of superb quality. *10 Lincoln Center Plaza | lincoln center.org | Subway 1 66th Street | ⊞ E–F5*

63 CHILDREN'S MUSEUM OF MANHATTAN 👶

A place for kids of up to ten years old to try out being an artist or a firefighter, learn new dances or do cool science experiments. *Daily 10am–5pm | 212 W 83rd Street | admission $15 | cmom.org | Subway 1 86th Street | ⊞ F2*

64 UPPER MANHATTAN

Upper Manhattan begins north of Central Park. The island becomes much thinner before reaching a park at its tip on 220th Street. The north has a lot to offer in terms of history and culture: African-American heritage in *Harlem*; Caribbean culture and cuisine in *Washington Heights*, and, in the middle of it all, is the expanding campus of the Ivy League Columbia University. *⊞ 0*

Unfinished but still magnificent: St John the Divine

65 ST JOHN THE DIVINE

The city's largest cathedral has enough space for a few surprises, not least for offering a warm welcome to animals. Every autumn hundreds of worshippers bring their pets to be blessed in the church, and, in spring, they bring their bicycles. There are roller discos, Halloween parties, readings and concerts, but plenty of "normal" religious services too. The cathedral was begun in 1892 and is still unfinished. One of the last works created by the artist Keith Haring is housed in a side chapel on the northern side. *Mon–Sat*

> **INSIDER TIP**
> **Wacky worship**

9.30am–5pm, Sun noon–5pm | 1047 Amsterdam Av. | admission $5 | stjohn divine.org | Subway 1 110th Street | ▢ 0

66 COLUMBIA UNIVERSITY

New York's Columbia University is one of only eight institutions that belong to the so-called "Ivy League" of elite universities. Take a wander through its main campus to get a sense of student life here. The university continues to expand: a new campus is being developed at the west end of 125th Street, which includes the excellent *Wallach Art Gallery (wallach.columbia. edu)*. *116th Street and Broadway | columbia.edu | Subway 1 116th Street | ▢ 0*

BROOKLYN

Despite being just a stone's throw from Manhattan, Brooklyn is like a different world – and it's one that's well worth exploring.

With a population of around 2.5 million, this borough would rate as one of the five largest *cities* in the USA by itself. As one of New York's five boroughs, Brooklyn has always had its own confident character and has never seen itself as in Manhattan's shadow. However, for the rest of the city, it was the aftermath of the 9/11 terror attacks that really put Brooklyn on the map; many Manhattan-ites desperately wanted to leave the island and Brooklyn's rents were still reasonably affordable. Since then, much of the city's cultural and night-life has migrated over the East River to Brooklyn, and rents in some areas are now at least as expensive as on Manhattan.

67 GREENPOINT

The district north of Williamsburg is nicknamed Little Poland, although nowadays you will find young couples, artists and students alongside the immigrants from Eastern Europe. It is a homely and inviting district with

Street art in Greenpoint

BROOKLYN

MANHATTAN

Greenpoint 67

68 Williamsburg

69 Dumbo

70 Brooklyn Heights

Fort Greene Park

Boerum Hill 71

71 Carroll Gardens

72 Red Hook

BROOKLYN

72 Gowanus

71 Park Slope

73 Brooklyn Museum

1 km
0.62 mi

Brooklyn Botanic Garden

---

shops selling Polish *kielbasa* sausages next door to excellent cafés and "farm-to-table" restaurants. *Also here is McCarren Park (nycgovparks.org/parks/mccarrenpark)*, which has lots of playgrounds and a beautiful renovated pool from 1936. *Subway G Greenpoint Av. |* ⌖ *K–L14*

68 WILLIAMSBURG

Once a summer bolthole for the wealthy, then a centre of industry, today Williamsburg is so popular with the young and successful that it has become synonymous with the word "hipster". Around Metropolitan Avenue, Grand Street and Bedford Avenue are an array of galleries, shops, restaurants and cafés that are great for Insta-friendly people-watching. Around 30,000 ultra-orthodox Jews from various sects still live here. You can learn about their lives on a fascinating tour led by someone who has left the

INSIDER TIP
Tour Orthodox Brooklyn

community *(friedavizel.com)*. Hipster Williamsburg has got so expensive that many people are now moving to neighbouring *Bushwick*. *St Nicholas Street* and *Troutman Street*, in particular, are focal points for New York's nightlife; by day, discover the street art of the "Bushwick Collective". *Subway L Bedford Av | ⚏ H–K16*

69 DUMBO

North of Brooklyn Heights is *Dumbo* – the acronym means *Down Under the Manhattan Bridge Overpass*. All day and all night, the trains will pause your conversation as they trundle overhead. This area has changed very rapidly from an industrial zone to a home for start-ups. Factories have been converted into apartments with amazing views of Manhattan and

> **INSIDER TIP**
> **Money shot of the Manhattan Bridge**

rents to match. In addition, there are galleries, design boutiques, bars and cafés. Don't miss the opportunity to take a photo from the corner of Washington and Water Street towards Manhattan. Cobblestones and brick buildings are in the foreground, while the Manhattan Bridge frames the Empire State Building in the background. *Subway F York Street | ⚏ D–E18*

70 BROOKLYN HEIGHTS

A flaneur's paradise – the borough's prettiest neighbourhood, with its well-maintained 19th-century brownstones, stretches out from the eastern edge of Brooklyn Bridge. Truman Capote, who lived at 70 Willow Street

in the 1950s, loved it so much he didn't want to leave. Stroll along *Pierrepoint* or *Remsen Street* west towards *Brooklyn Heights Promenade* to find out why this area is still so popular: the amazing views of Manhattan and the Statue of Liberty! And lower down along the river bank is *Brooklyn Bridge Park*, with its miles of paths, sports pitches, picnic benches, playgrounds and ice-cream stands. *Subway 2, 3 Clark Street | ⚏ H20*

71 CARROLL GARDENS, BOERUM HILL & PARK SLOPE

Today, this once-seedy part of Brooklyn is a sought-after area with great restaurants, delightful designer boutiques and protected heritage houses. Young families, hip couples and wealthy single people have taken up residence in the brownstones in Carroll Gardens, Boerum Hill and Park Slope. Writers, including Paul Auster and Jonathan Lethem, live in these districts and have documented their changing demographics in their novels. These are great places to wander around. If you see cool clothes or books left on steps or fences outside people's houses, feel free to pick them up. *Subway F, G Carroll Street | ⚏ G–K 22–25*

> **INSIDER TIP**
> **Vintage and free!**

72 RED HOOK & GOWANUS

A little further on and everything changes again. Red Hook and Gowanus were once home to factories and a port, and although there are many luxury apartments here too,

Down under the Manhattan Bridge: Dumbo's most famous view

these areas have retained some of their gruff charm. The canal in Gowanus was polluted by local factories for so long that it is still one of the most toxic bodies of water in the USA. However, a big clean-up operation has begun, and you can now kayak along it *(gowanuscanal.org)* – a slightly dubious but certainly different way to see the city

Red Hook was immortalised in the classic film *On the Waterfront* – for which Marlon Brando received an Oscar in 1955. It was subsequently settled by artists and later overtaken by real-estate agents. And it is where cruise ships dock when they visit New York. The best shops, restaurants and cafés are in the area around *Van Brunt Street*, and don't miss out on a visit to the freshly renovated *Pioneer Works* art centre *(Wed–Sun 1–8pm | 159 Pioneer Street | free admission| pioneerworks.org). Subway A, C, F, G Jay Street-MetroTech, then bus B61 to the end of Van Brunt Street | ⌑ E–J24*

73 BROOKLYN MUSEUM

New York's second-largest museum (after the Metropolitan Museum) is housed in an imposing art nouveau building in Brooklyn, dating from 1897. The collection provides an overview of art from the United States and is complemented by an exciting programme of special exhibitions. Right next to the museum is Prospect Park, Brooklyn's answer to Central Park, complete with botanical garden, zoo, carousel and ice rink. *Wed–Sun 11am–6pm | 200 Eastern Parkway | admission $16 | brooklynmuseum. org | Subway 2, 3 Eastern Parkway | ⌑ N25*

OTHER SIGHTS

74 HARLEM

Harlem is the centre of African-American culture in New York. You will rarely feel so underdressed as you will wandering around this area. Take some time to explore the streets with their wonderful old buildings, such as *Astor Row (W 130th Street/between 5th and Lenox Av.)* and *Strivers' Row (West 138th and 139th Street/ between Adam Clayton Powell Jr. Blvd and Frederick Douglass Blvd)*. You will find restaurants with delicious Somali and Ethiopian cuisine, nightclubs where Duke Ellington and Aretha Franklin once played and extremely cool shops. *125th Street* is Harlem's centre and home to the *Apollo Theater (253 W 125th Street | apollotheater. org | see p. 122)* – a centre for African-American culture. Get tickets to *Amateur Night (Wed 7.30pm)*, New York's toughest and most entertaining talent show. There are 🦜 Gospel services across Harlem on Sunday mornings, but those at the biggest churches are now so popular with tourists that you'll have to get there very early to get in. It can be more fun to stroll through the streets. keeping an ear out for the unmistakeable sound of Gospel-singing in order to find one of the smaller churches. *Subway 2, 3, A–D 125th Street | ⌑ 0*

75 MORRIS-JUMEL MANSION & SYLVAN TERRACE

Washington Heights is Manhattan's highest (and narrowest) point. There is always a cooling breeze in this area, even in summer. The heights were once popular with exiles from Nazi Germany. Today it is more a centre for Caribbean culture in the city and is home to the oldest building for miles around – the *Morris-Jumel Mansion*, where George Washington, the first US president, briefly resided in 1776. Next to it is one of the city's prettiest historic streets, *Sylvan Terrace*; don't miss it. *Subway A, C 163rd Street |* 🚇 0

⁷⁶ WAVE HILL

A break in the Bronx. Wave Hill is a grand 19th-century house with an amazing garden that is today open to the public. Pick up a piece of the famous carrot cake from *Lloyd's Carrot Cake (6087 Broadway | lloydscarrotcake. com)* and head to Wave Hill, where you can munch it in one of the meadows, with great views of the Hudson River and the hills of New Jersey beyond. *Tue–Sun 10am–5.30pm | admission $10, free on Sun | W 249th Street/Independence Av. | wavehill.org | Subway 1 242nd Street, then take the free shuttlebus |* 🚇 0

INSIDER TIP
Carrot cake with a view

⁷⁷ BRONX ZOO & NEW YORK BOTANICAL GARDEN

The Bronx is also home to the city's 🐵 best *zoo (daily 10am–4.30pm, longer hours at weekends Apr–Nov | admission from $26.95, or by voluntary donation on Wed | 2300 Southern Blvd | bronxzoo.com)* where the animals mostly live in huge enclosures. If a visit to the zoo leaves you wanting more nature, the *New York Botanical Garden (Tue–Sun 10am–6pm | 2900 Southern Blvd | admission from $30 | nybg.org)* is directly opposite. *Subway 2,5 Pelham Pkwy |* 🚇 0

Bar life in Harlem

78 BRONX MUSEUM

This small museum sits on Grand Concourse, the Bronx's central street. It hosts lots of temporary exhibitions on the history of the area and its diverse culture – and they are all free! If you want to see more of the Bronx's artistic heritage, head to the bold photography museum, the *Bronx Documentary Center (bronxdoc.org)*. *Wed–Sun 1–6pm | 1040 Grand Concourse | bronxmuseum.org | Subway 4, B, D 161st Street/Yankee Stadium | ○ 1–2 hrs | ▥ 0*

79 MOMA PS1 🐖

The second branch of the Museum of Modern Art is housed in an old primary school in Queens and shows contemporary art. It holds cool temporary exhibitions and popular parties at the weekend. *Long Island City*, where the museum is located, is the fastest-growing district in the USA. There are new skyscrapers on every corner. If you have made the journey out here make sure to wander through *Gantry Plaza State Park* – it has playgrounds, lots of green space and free yoga classes with amazing views of the Midtown skyline. *Sun, Mon, Thu noon–6pm, Fri, Sat noon–8pm | 22–25 Jackson Av. | admission free, donations welcome | momaps1.org | Subway E, M, G 7 Court Square 23rd Street | ○ 2 hrs | ▥ L10*

80 MUSEUM OF THE MOVING IMAGE

Try out being a cameraman, sound engineer or animator in the heart of Queens. You can shoot short

animations, try out sound effects, make flick books or just watch films for hours and hours. *Tue 2–6pm, Fri 2–8pm, Sat, Sun noon–6pm | 36–01 35th Av./37th Street | admission $15, 🐖 free 2–6pm Thu | movingimage. us | Subway M, R Steinway Street | ○ 1–2 hrs | ▥ 0*

81 LOUIS ARMSTRONG MUSEUM

Despite probably being the most famous trumpeter in the world, Louis Armstrong and his wife Lucille lived in this modest house in Queens until his death in 1971. Despite being globally renowned, Armstrong most enjoyed playing his trumpet for kids in this neighbourhood. The house looks exactly as it did when the Armstrongs lived there. *Thu–Sun 11am–4pm |*

New York shows off its green and pleasant side at the Botanical Garden in the Bronx

34 56 107th Street | admission incl. tour $15 | louisarmstronghouse.org | Subway 7 103rd Street-Corona Plaza | ▥ 0

82 FLUSHING MEADOWS – CORONA PARK

This was the venue for the World Fair in 1939/40. Today it is home to the New York Mets Baseball Team and hosts the elite of world tennis in August, who battle it out for a trophy in the annual US Open. The park around the famous globe is great for a stroll. Nearby is the 🏛 *Queens Museum (Wed-Fri noon-5pm, Sat, Sun 11am-5pm | admission free | queensmuseum.org)*, with its fascinating scale model of the city, and the 🏛 *New York Hall of Science (Thu,* *Sat, Sun 10am-5pm, Fri 2-5pm | 47-01 111th Street | admission $14 | nysci.org)*. Hungry? Take subway Line 7 for one stop to the end of the line. *Flushing* is New York's newest Chinatown and has lots of great restaurants. *Subway 7 Mets Willets Point | ▥ 0*

83 GOVERNORS ISLAND 🏛

For 200 years Governors Island was closed to the public, but now anyone can come here to laze in one of the 50 hammocks or whoosh down a 20m slide. There are no cars, but plenty of nature, free concerts and other activities. If you want to stay longer, glamping is available *(collective retreats.com/governors-island)*. *Sun-Thu 7am-6pm, Fri, Sat 7am-10pm |*

Take the subway to the beach! Coney Island awaits

ferry from the tip of Manhattan, also from Brooklyn at weekends and public holidays | govisland.com | Subway 1 South Ferry | ⊞ D–F21–22

84 SNUG HARBOR

Most tourists who take the ferry across to Staten Island turn around in the ferry dock and head straight back across on the next boat. There is no doubt that the view of the skyline and the Statue of Liberty from the ferry is superb, but don't underestimate Staten Island!

Residents here often say they are the "fifth and forgotten wheel" (borough) of the city. This is beginning to change, and it is partly thanks to attractions like Snug Harbor. Once a retirement home for sailors (which counted writer Herman Melville's brother among its directors), it has now been turned into a large art and cultural centre with an excellent history museum, a 😍 kids' museum and lots of green space. The site is open from dawn until dusk, but it is best to look up the opening times and prices for individual museums and attractions online. 1000 Richmond Terrace | snug-harbor.org | take Bus S40 from the ferry quay | ⊞ 0

85 ALICE AUSTEN HOUSE

Alice Austen was a New York photographer in the 19th century. Her old house in Staten Island has been turned into a charming museum with excellent exhibitions, and its garden has incredible views over towards Manhattan and the Verrazza Narrows Bridge. Mar–Dec Tue–Sat noon–5pm | 2 Hylan Blvd | admission $10 | aliceausten.org | take Bus S51 from the quay | ⊞ 0

🎏 CONEY ISLAND & BRIGHTON BEACH 🎭

Take the subway to the beach! There is an amusement park on the promenade here with a ferris wheel and roller coaster. If the weather is good, you can also take a dip in the Atlantic before sunbathing on the beach. If it is raining, have a hot dog at *Nathan's* (the place that apparently invented them!) or go to the *New York Aquarium (daily 10am–5pm | 602 Surf Av. | admission from $26.95 | nyaquarium.com).*

Follow the wooden boardwalk to the west to reach Brighton Beach aka "Little Odessa". Immigrants from across the former Soviet Union have settled here. Make sure to leave some appetite as the neighbourhood is full of cheap and delicious restaurants and bakeries. *Subway D, F, Q, N Coney Island, Stillwell Av. | ▭ 0*

DAY TRIP

🎏 HUDSON RIVER VALLEY

200 km to Rhinebeck/3 hrs (car)

A day trip in a rental car north along the Hudson River through the hilly and forested landscape comes highly recommended. Follow Route 9 to *Kykuit* and the imposing *Rockefeller Estate (May–Sept Sat, Sun, Oct–Nov Wed–Mon | 381 N Broadway | Sleepy Hollow | admission with tour from $20 | short.travel/new11)* where the art collection of former Vice President Nelson B. Rockefeller awaits you.

Further north in *Hyde Park*, you can take in the 54-room Renaissance mansion of renowned 19th-century railroad magnate Frederick W. Vanderbilt, *Vanderbilt Mansion (daily 7am–8pm | nps.gov/vama)* along with the stately home of former President Franklin D. Roosevelt *(daily 7am–8pm | nps.gov/hofr).* Hyde Park is also the location of the *Culinary Institute of America (ciachef.edu | $–$$$)* where the best young chefs in the country serve food in four restaurants (reservation essential!).

Viticulture also thrives in the Hudson Valley; its warm, humid climate is ideal for excellent dry white wines, e.g. *Millbrook Vineyards (millbrookwine.com).* To end your day, pop into the picture-perfect town of *Rhinebeck*, which dates back to 1686. ▭ 0

Who invented the hotdog? Nathan's, apparently

EATING & DRINKING

So much cultural heritage, so many cuisines! New York offers you the chance to scoff your way around the world without leaving the city!

There are all sorts of eateries in this city, from snack stands to Michelin-starred restaurants, serving everything from Korean *kimchi*, Japanese sushi and Mexican burritos to lobster from Maine or a juicy steak. For good-value food around the clock, head to a food truck, a local Chinese restaurant, a pizza joint or a traditional diner.

Almost everywhere in the USA, you should wait to be shown to a

You'll find all the venues in this chapter on the pull-out map 📖

Mulberry Street is the heart of Little Italy

free table rather than sitting wherever you choose. Tap water is nearly always offered for free, and your glass will be frequently topped up. Serving staff will expect a tip – basic waiter pay is shockingly low, so staff depend on tips to supplement their wages. To calculate a fair tip, it is a good idea to double the amount of VAT you have paid on a bill.

Twice a year the city holds a "Restaurant Week" (usually in January and then in summer). During these weeks, you can eat lunch or dinner for a reasonable price at even the top restaurants in town (*nycgo.com/restaurant-week*).

WHERE TO EAT IN NEW YORK

Barney Greengrass

Nougatine at Jean Georges ★

Central Park

West 57th Street

Pure ★

NEW YORK

West 42nd Street

NEW JERSEY

West 34th Street

West 23rd Street

Buddakan ★

East 34th Street

East 42nd Street

5th Avenue

Madison Avenue

Park Ave

EAST VILLAGE
Almost every building houses a bar, restaurant or café

East 14th Street

TRIBECA
Industrial history, celeb hangouts and cool restaurants

MANHATTAN

Astor Place M

M 1 Avenue

Avenue A

Avenue B

Avenue C

Avenue D

Canal Street

Broadway

Bowery

Chrystie Street

Allen Street

East Houston St.

Katz's Delicatessen ★

Grand Banks ★

Franklin Street

Park Place M

M City Hall

Centre Street

Nom Wah Tea Parlor ★

M East Broadway

FDR Drive

CHINATOWN
Authenic Asian delicacies from all over the continent

York Street

BROOKLYN

MARCO POLO HIGHLIGHTS

★ **NOUGATINE AT JEAN GEORGES**
Heavenly modern French-American cuisine from master chef Jean-Georges Vongerichten ➤ p.74

★ **GRAND BANKS**
Oysters at sundown on an old cod trawler ➤ p.76

★ **BUDDAKAN**
Prize-wining restaurant with OTT design and delicious food ➤ p.76

★ **BARNEY GREENGRASS**
Quintessential New York deli – don't miss it ➤ p.76

★ **PURE**
Delicious Thai noodles (and much more) in this charming restaurant ➤ p.78

★ **NOM WAH TEA PARLOR**
Hip crowd, delicious dumplings ➤ p.78

★ **KATZ'S DELICATESSEN**
The best pastrami sandwiches in town, made famous in the film *When Harry Met Sally* ➤ p.79, p.138

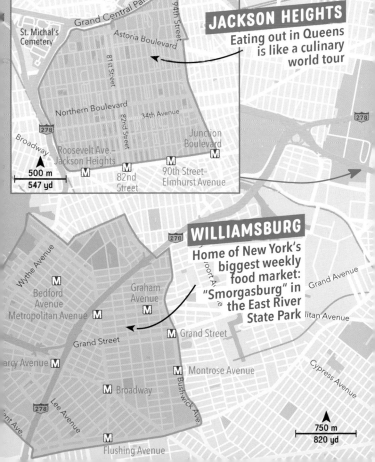

JACKSON HEIGHTS
Eating out in Queens is like a culinary world tour

WILLIAMSBURG
Home of New York's biggest weekly food market: "Smorgasburg" in the East River State Park

CAFÉS

1 ALMAR
Long wooden tables where you can enjoy a panino with prosciutto and fresh mozzarella or just a cappuccino? Mostly organic too. *Closed Sun | 111 Front Street | tel. 1 718 8 55 52 88 | almardumbo.com | Subway F York Street | Dumbo | ⌑ E18*

2 AMY'S BREAD 🏵
One of the cupcakes in this bakery that uses regional, organic ingredients is called "Devil's Food". The bread and cake are also devilishly good, while the coffee, breakfast baguettes and jam and lunch sandwiches are heavenly. *Daily | 672 9th Av., between 46th and 47th Street | tel. 1 212 9 77 26 70 | amysbread.com | Subway 1 50th Street | Hell's Kitchen | ⌑ E7*

3 DOUGHNUT PLANT 🚩
Doughnut connoisseurs swear that this is where to get the best in the city. The delicious creations come in all shape, sizes and flavours! *Closed Mon, Tue | 245 Flatbush Av. | tel. 1 212 5 05 37 00 | doughnutplant.com | Subway B, Q 7th Av. | Downtown Brooklyn | ⌑ L23*

4 ABOUT COFFEE
This small chain of coffeeshops is run with love and style by an Egyptian resident of Long Island. One of the most welcoming branches is located close to Central Park and the American Museum of Natural History. *Daily | 445 Columbus Av. | tel. 1 646 8 52 68 12 | aboutcoffee.nyc | Subway B, C 81st Street-Museum of Natural History | Upper West Side | ⌑ G3*

5 INTELLIGENTSIA
In this little oasis in fast-paced Chelsea, the superb coffee comes from an old Citroën minibus. It is the High Line Hotel's coffee bar and is not big but there is plenty of space outside. *Daily from 7am | 180 10th Av./between 20th and 21st Street | tel. 1 212 9 33 97 36 | thehighlinehotel.com/ intelligentsia | Subway C, E 23rd Street | Chelsea | ⌑ C10*

6 VENIERO'S
Loud and crowded with unmissable treats – since 1894. **INSIDER TIP** Buy some *dolci* for your breakfast before you leave! **Stock up on treats** *Daily | 342 E 11th Street/between 1st and 2nd Av. | tel. 1 212 6 74 70 70 | Subway L 1st Av. | East Village | ⌑ E13*

7 DOMINIQUE ANSEL BAKERY
Dominique Ansel became globally famous when he mixed a croissant with a donut to create a *cronut*. Even when these trendy treats are sold out (normally by noon), a visit to his shop will be rewarded by something indulgent and delicious. *Daily | 189 Spring Street | tel. 1 212 2 19 27 73 | dominiqueansel.com | Subway C, E Spring Street | SoHo | ⌑ C14*

RESTAURANTS $$$

8 CARBONE
Its name gives the secret away: criminally good Italian pasta. One variant

Bananas, pecan nuts, glaze – a classic New York snack from Doughnut Plant

comes served with lobster, clams and caper sauce. Beloved by critics. *Mon, Tue evening only | 181 Thompson Street/between Bleecker and W Houston Street | tel. 1 212 2 54 30 00 | carbonenewyork.com | Subway B, D, F, M Broadway-Lafayette | Greenwich Village | ⫏ C13*

⑨ CHURRASCARIA PLATAFORMA

Meat – and plenty of it – grilled to perfection. A Brazilian steak house with an excellent salad bar. *Daily | Belvedere Hotel | 316 W 49th Street | tel. 1 212 2 45 05 05 | plataforma online.com | Subway C 50 Street | Hell's Kitchen | ⫏ E7*

⑩ CRAFT

Critics love Tom Colicchio who is behind this upmarket restaurant. Selected farmers work closely with the chef to ensure that only the finest ingredients are served. *Daily | 43 E 19th Street | tel. 1 212 7 80 08 80 | craftrestaurant.com | Subway R, 6 23rd Street | Gramercy/Flatiron District | ⫏ E11*

⑪ ELEVEN MADISON PARK

This restaurant has been declared the best in the world several times and has three Michelin stars for its seasonal, regional cooking. The latest innovation from Swiss master chef Daniel Humm is a completely vegan menu, available for $335 in the dining room or in a smaller format at the bar for $195. *Dinner only Sun–Fri, lunch & dinner Sat | 11 Madison Av. | tel. 1 212 8 89 09 05 | elevenmadisonpark.com | Subway R, 6 23rd Street | Flatiron District | ⫏ E11*

⑫ NOBU

Star chef Nobu Matsuhisa is responsible for popularising fine Japanese cuisine in the USA and has since built a culinary empire here. *Daily | 195 Broadway | tel. 1 212 2 19 05 00 | noburestaurants.com | Subway 2, 3, 4, 5, A, C, J, Z Fulton Street | Financial District | ⫏ B15*

13 NOUGATINE AT JEAN GEORGES ⭐

Wherever Jean-Georges Vongerichten opens a restaurant, the "in" crowd follows. Whether Maine lobster or pork chops with prosciutto, the food is top-notch. *Daily | 1 Central Park W | tel. 1 212 2 99 39 00 | jean-georges restaurant.com | Subway 1, A, B, C, D 59th Street-Columbus Circle | Lincoln Square | ⚏ F6*

14 PETER LUGER

A 130-year-old steakhouse which entices its guests with charm… and large portions. For 30 years this has been voted the best steakhouse in New York. Credit cards not accepted. *Daily | 178 Broadway/between Driggs and Bedford Street | tel. 1 718 3 87 74 00 | peterluger.com | Subway J Marcy Av. | Brooklyn | ⚏ J17*

15 15 EAST @ TOCQUEVILLE

Smart contemporary American cuisine that fuses French and Japanese elements to produce unique and delicious dishes. *Daily | 1 E 15th Street | tel. 1 212 6 47 15 15 | 15east tocqueville-nyc.com | Subway L, N, Q, R, 4, 5, 6 14 Street-Union Square | Union Square | ⚏ D12*

16 ENOTECA MARIA

Like at your grandma's – for real! This wonderful restaurant is walking distance from the Staten Island Ferry. Its chefs are not highly trained pros but grandmothers, and the food they produce is as good as any Michelin-rated eatery. The atmosphere is grand and cosy in equal measure. *Fri–Sun | 27 Hyatt Street | tel. 1 718 4 47 27 77 | enotecamaria.com | Staten Island Ferry | Staten Island | ⚏ 0*

Book in advance to sample the finest Japanese delicacies at Nobu

Today's Specials

Snacks

BAGEL
Choose from different varieties, including sesame, olives or raisins, and then select your filling: peppers, cream cheese, smoked salmon, or something else

CRAB CAKES
Deep-fried or grilled crab is combined with many different ingredients to create a unique snack

Starters

CLAM CHOWDER
Seafood soup – either New England (white) or Manhattan (red) style

OYSTERS
A touch of salt? Lemon? Chilli sauce? Ketchup? How do you slurp yours?

Main courses

LUMBERJACK
A huge breakfast of eggs, bacon, potatoes and pancakes

BURGER
America's biggest culinary export still tastes best in its home country

PASTRAMI SANDWICH
Seasoned smoked beef stacked on bread

REUBEN SANDWICH
Corned beef, sauerkraut, Russian sauce and Swiss cheese on rye bread

LOBSTER
This majestic ingredient is served in every way imaginable in New York

NEW YORK STRIP STEAK
Delicious fatty sirloin steak beloved in the city

TURKEY
Traditionally served at Thanksgiving with cranberries, gravy and sweet potatoes

Desserts

CHEESECAKE
New York's most famous dessert comes in all kinds of flavours

BLACK-AND-WHITE COOKIES
Chocolate and vanilla discs of deliciousness

BROWNIES
You will be amazed how many different types of brownies New York cafés can produce

RESTAURANTS $$

17 BRYANT PARK GRILL

A popular spot for fashionistas to eat seafood and BBQ. Brunch on weekends from 11.30am. *Daily | 25 W 40th Street/between 5th and 6th Av. | tel. 1 212 8 40 65 00 | bryantparkgrillnyc. com | Subway B, D, F, M 42nd Street | Midtown West | ▢ F8*

18 GRAND BANKS ⭐

Try the excellent seafood, from oysters to mussels, on this erstwhile cod trawler on the Hudson. *Lunchtime only, daily Apr–Oct | Pier 25 Hudson River Park | tel. 1 212 6 60 63 12 | crewny.com/grand-banks | Subway 1 Franklin Street | Tribeca | ▢ A15*

19 BUDDAKAN ⭐

Opulent furnishings and excellent modern food, Budakkan has won many prizes for its exciting Asian food and over the top décor with chandeliers hanging above the banquet tables. *Evenings only | 75 9th Av./16th Street | tel. 1 212 9 89 66 99 | budda kannyc.com | Subway A, C, E, L 14th Street | Meatpacking District | ▢ C11*

20 BARNEY GREENGRASS ⭐

"If God made anything better, he kept it for himself" said Anthony Bourdain of the signature "nova and eggs" in this classic deli. A wonderful piece of old New York. *Closed Mon | 541 Amsterdam Av./86th Street | tel. 1 212 7 24 47 07 | barneygreengrass.com | Subway 1 86th Street | Upper West Side | ▢ G2*

21 COPPELIA

This diner serves delicious Cuban food 24 hours a day. Delight in their fish tacos, empanadas and guacamole. *207 W 14th Street | near 7th Av. | tel. 1 212 8 58 50 01 | ilovecoppelia.com | Subway 1, 2, 3 14th Street | Chelsea | ▢ C11*

22 TAP

It's summer; the city is so hot and humid that it has taken away your appetite, but you still need energy for sightseeing. In that case, Tap's cool, delicious and healthy bowls with acai berries are the answer! *Daily | 685 3rd Av./43rd Street | tel. 1 646 4 78 79 80 | tapnyc.com | Subway S, 4, 5, 6, 7 Grand Central-42nd Street | Midtown | ▢ G9*

INSIDER TIP Sightseeing superfood

23 FETTE SAU

Organic hearty BBQ food with craft beer to wash it down in trendy Williamsburg. Rustic and cosy. *Closed Mon | 354 Metropolitan Av. | tel. 1 718 9 63 34 04 | fettesaubbq.com | Subway L Bedford Avenue | Williamsburg | ▢ J16*

24 HAN BAT

Authentic food in Korea-town. Rice with eggs, meat and vegetables from the hot stone grill, but you can also order offal, tongue or the rice dish *bi bim bab*. *Daily | 53 W 35 Street/5th Av. | tel. 1 212 6 29 55 88 | hanbat35. com | Subway B, D, F, M, N, O, R 34th Street-Herald Square | Koreatown | ▢ E9*

25 BURGER JOINT

Yes, you are in the right place, even though you're standing outside the Thompson Hotel! Go inside, head to the left of the reception desk then to the right and – surprise! You are in one of the coolest and tastiest burger joints in town. *Daily | 119 W 56th Street | Tel. 1*

INSIDER TIP
Classy burgers

1 212 5 82 51 00 | marearestaurant. com/new-york | Subway A–D, 1 59th Street-Columbus Circle | Columbus Circle | ▢ F6

27 JG MELON

A cosy corner bar that serves some of the best burgers in the city, accompanied by round, crinkle-cut "cottage fried potatoes". *Daily | 1291 3rd*

It's hard to believe that Burger Joint is hidden away in a luxury hotel

212 708 7414 | burgerjointny.com | Subway F 57th Street | Theatre District | ▢ F6

26 MAREA

Taste of the sea? This excellent Italian restaurant serves delectable flounder, monkfish, mussels and lobsters. *240 Central Park South/Broadway | tel.*

Av./74th Street | tel. 1 212 7 44 05 85 | jgmelon-nyc.com | Subway Q 72nd Street | Upper East Side | ▢ J5

28 MOMOFUKU SSÄM BAR

Popular, hip restaurant for fans of superbly prepared meat: veal, lamb, ham and bacon, all prepared Asian-style. *Closed Mon | 89 South Street/*

Pier 17 | tel. 1 212 2 54 35 00 | ssam bar.momofuku.com | Subway 2, 3 Wall Street | South Street Seaport | ⌑ C17

29 GRAND CENTRAL OYSTER BAR

Knock back an oyster in a station? Really? Sure! This super-stylish New York institution serves fish soups and some alternatives to seafood if it's not your thing. But oysters are rightly the main event! *Closed Sat, Sun | Grand Central Terminal, Lower Level between Vanderbilt and Lexington Av. | tel. 1 212 4 90 66 50 | oysterbarny.com | Subway 4–7 Grand Central | Midtown East | ⌑ F9*

30 VINEGAR HILL HOUSE

There aren't many restaurants in this

INSIDER TIP
Brunch highlight

out-of-the-way district, but this is one of the best. Don't miss the legendary sourdough pancakes, served for weekend brunch. *Daily | 72 Hudson Av. | tel. 1 718 5 22 10 18 | vinegarhillhouse.com | Subway F York Street | Vinegar Hill | ⌑ F18*

31 PURE ★

Take a trip to Asia for an hour or so. The recipes in this delightful, small cook-house in Hell's Kitchen (just 35 covers!) were brought back from Thailand by Vanida Bank. *Closed Sun | 766 9th Av./between 51st and 52nd Street | tel. 1 212 5 81 09 99 | pure thaicookhouse.com | Subway C, E 50th Street | Hell's Kitchen | ⌑ E6*

32 NOM WAH TEA PARLOR ★

This Chinatown institution is now run by the long-time owner's nephew. Order and enjoy little bites of dim sum deliciousness and other authentic dishes, all served with aromatic tea. *Closed Wed | 13 Doyers Street | tel. 1 212 9 62 60 47 | nomwah.com | Subway J, M, Z Canal Street | Chinatown | ⌑ C16*

33 LA MORADA

A family-run restaurant which justifies a trip to the Bronx! The dishes made using mole sauces from Oaxaca are particularly good. The politically engaged owner is from the region, and his restaurant comes with a small library and toys for kids. *Mon–Wed | 308 Willis Av. | tel. 1 718 2 92 02 35 | lamoradanyc.com | Subway 6 3rd Av./ 138th Street | Bronx | ⌑ 0*

34 ROBERT

A unique New York experience in the Museum of Art and Design. Lounge on one of the comfortable couches or order a tender New York strip steak and take in the incredible views over Central Park and Columbus Circle. *Closed Mon | 2 Columbus Circle | tel. 1 212 2 99 77 30 | robertnyc.com | Subway A–D, 1 59th Street-Columbus Circle | Columbus Circle | ⏏ F6*

35 RUSS & DAUGHTERS CAFÉ

Jewish treats from eastern Europe served in old New York style. Matzo ball soup, borsht and latkes (potato cakes) with caviar. *Thu–Sun | 127 Orchard Street/between Rivington and Delancey Street | tel. 1 212 4 75 48 80 | russanddaughterscafe.com | Subway F Delancey Street | Lower East Side | ⏏ E15*

36 KATZ'S DELICATESSEN ⭐

Remember the most famous scene in the rom-com *When Harry Met Sally.* The one where Meg Ryan fakes an orgasm while eating with Billy Crystal? It was filmed here, and there is even a plaque on the table where it happened. Katz's has been serving the very best pastrami sandwiches for over 125 years. They are enormous, so don't be afraid to share. *Daily | 205 E Houston Street | tel. 1 212 2 54 22 46 | katzdelicatessen.com | Subway F 2nd Avenue | Chinatown | ⏏ E14*

Make tracks to Grand Central Terminal's Oyster Bar

37 ANABLE BASIN

A pleasant beer garden with reasonable prices and a perfect view of the New York skyline? It doesn't exist! Yes, it does! *Daily (cash only) | 4-40 44th Drive | tel. 1 718 4 33 92 69 | anable basin.com | Subway E, M, G, 7 Court Square-23rd Street | Long Island City | ⊞ J-K9*

RESTAURANTS $

38 MEL

Do you see the queue? Then you know you're in the right place. Mel grinds its own flour in order to create some of the best baked goods in the city, both sweet and savoury. While you tuck in, indulge in some people-watching on ultra-hip Dimes Square. *Thu-Sun | 1 Ludlow Street | tel. 1 917 3 82 02 78 | melthebakery.com | Subway F East Broadway | Lower East Side | ⊞ E16*

39 CHUKO

The ramen (savoury Japanese noodle soup) here is simply fantastic. *Daily | 565 Vanderbilt Av./Dean Street | tel. 1347 4 25 95 70 | chukobk.com | Subway A, C Clinton-Washington Av. | Brooklyn | ⊞ M23*

40 DOS TOROS TAQUERIA

Simple, fast, cheap. This chain serves tacos, burritos and quesadillas. It aims to operate sustainably by using local food and composting leftovers. There are multiple branches, including *11 Carmine Street, corner Bleecker Street | tel. 1 212 6 27 20 51 | Subway A, C, E, B, D, F, M W 4th Street | dostoros.com | West Village | ⊞ C13*

41 BIRRIA-LANDIA 🚚

Even the *New York Times* raves about this food truck! Dip tacos into the signature sauce, tuck in and enjoy the fiesta atmosphere underneath the Queens flyover. *Daily | 77-99 Roosevelt Av. | tel. 1 347 2 83 21 62 | birralandia.com | Subway 7, E, F, M, R Jackson Heights-Roosevelt Av. | Jackson Heights | ⊞ 0*

42 VESELKA 🚩

This New York institution serves good value delicious eastern European food. Delicious dumplings and *borsht* feature alongside burgers and sandwiches. *Daily | 144 2nd Av. | tel. 1 212 2 28 96 82 | eselka.com | Subway 6 Astor Place | East Village | ⊞ E13*

43 LEXINGTON CANDY SHOP

This welcoming corner diner is like something out of a Woody Allen movie – and, yes, Allen did in fact film some scenes here. *Daily | 1226 Lexington Av. | tel. 1 212 2 88 00 57 | lexingtoncandyshop.com | Subway 4, 5, 6 86th Street | Upper East Side | ⊞ J4*

44 WU'S WONTON KING

Peking ducks hang in the shop window enticing locals to meet here for family meals and special occasions. Settle yourself at one of the round tables and tuck in! *Daily | 165 E Broadway | tel. 1 212 4 77 11 11 | wuswontonking.com | Subway F East Broadway | Lower East Side | ⊞ E16*

The staff at Katz's make the most famous pastrami sandwiches in the city

45 KOPITIAM

Fancy a Malaysian meal? This relaxed and friendly diner allows you to take a deep dive into one of Asia's most exciting cuisines, which incorporates elements from Thailand, China and India. From milky toast at breakfast to rice noodles in the evening, everything here is great. *Daily | 151 East Broadway | tel. 1 646 6 09 37 85 | kopitiamnyc.com | Subway F East Broadway | Chinatown | ⊞ E16*

46 LORELEY

The imported beers are what make this German beer garden – run by renowned DJ Michael Momm – such a popular choice. It's also a good place to watch European football. *Daily | 7 Rivington Street/between Bowery and Chrystie Street | tel. 1 212 2 53 70 77 | loreleynyc.com | Subway F, M 2nd Av. | Lower East Side | ⊞ D14*

47 HALAL GUYS

When Hurricane Sandy wreaked havoc on New York in 2012, the city was virtually deserted and most shops did not open. The Halal Guys, however, carried on serving their delicious food throughout. This stubborn bravery allowed these three Egyptian immigrants to turn a simple halal kebab stand into a global empire which is popular with New Yorkers from all backgrounds. There are now branches all over the USA (and indeed in other countries too), but the original and the best is still here. *Daily | W 53rd/6th Av. | thehalalguys.com | Subway B, D, E 7th Av. | Midtown | ⊞ E6*

48 99 CENTS FRESH PIZZA 🚩

Eating a quick slice of pizza on the way to a meeting or to see friends is part of life in New York. Everyone here knows that, if all else fails, there will always be pizza. If your holiday budget is beginning to feel stretched, get a dollar slice and tuck into the cheesy goodness. *Daily | 71 2nd Av. | tel. 1 212 967 33 10 | 99centsfreshpizzanyc.com | Subway F 2nd Av.* | *East Village | ⊞ E13*

49 AREPA LADY

The Arepa Lady is a judge who came to New York from Columbia and who made a name for herself selling delicious corn flatbreads from a small truck, long before she had a restaurant in Jackson Heights. Fortunately, the *arepas* served in the restaurant still taste as good as the originals. *Daily | 77–17 37th Av. | tel. 1 917 7 45 11 11 | Subway 7, E, F, M, R Jackson Heights–Roosevelt Av.* | *Jackson Heights | ⊞ 0*

50 SHABU-TATSU

Do-it-yourself dinner. At this fondue joint, you can fry paper-thin slices of top-class beef fillet from Japan. *Daily | 216 E 10th Street | tel. 1 212 4 77 29 72 | shabutatsu.com | Subway 6 Astor Place | East Village | ⊞ E13*

51 SHAKE SHACK ⚑

Join the queue for the best burgers, hot dogs and milkshakes at the chain's original shop

INSIDER TIP
Worth the wait

in Madison Square Park in the shadow of the Flatiron Building. Owner Danny Meyer's subsequent success began here. Having to queue is all part of the experience. *Daily | tel. 1 212 8 89 66 00 | shakeshack.com | Subway 6 23rd Street | Flatiron District | ⊞ E11*

Queue up for a taste of Shake Shack's burgers and hotdogs

52 SILVER RICE

Yes, even paper cups can be beautiful if they are filled with sticky rice, sesame seeds, raw tuna or salmon, slices of avocado, strips of cucumber and spicy mayonnaise. All of which tastes much better eaten outdoors. *Daily | 638 Park Place | Brooklyn | tel. 1 718 3 98 82 00 | silverrice.com | Subway 2, 3, 4, 5 Franklin Av. | Crown Heights | ▥ 0*

53 SMORGASBURG

At this huge open-air market, munch your way through the stalls selling sandwiches, buttermilk-fried chicken, home-pickled gherkins and home-made ice cream. *April–Oct, Fri: Fulton Street/Church Street | Subway 1 WTC Cortlandt | Financial District | ▥ B16; Sat: E River State Park/Kent Av. and N 7th Street | Williamsburg | Subway L Bedford Av. | Williamsburg | ▥ H–J14-15; Sun: Breeze Hill/Prospect Park | Subway B, Q Prospect Park | Prospect Park | ▥ 0 | smorgasburg.com*

54 XI'AN FAMOUS FOODS

If Manhattan's Chinatown isn't enough for you, then head to Flushing where you can eat your way around Asia at any number of restaurants. Start at Xi'An, which has now developed into a small chain with branches in other parts of the city. *Closed Sun | 41-10 Main Street | tel. 1 212 7 86 20 68 | xianfoods.com | Subway / Flushing-Main Street | Flushing | ▥ 0*

55 SYLVIA'S RESTAURANT

Southern cuisine is still served up in the Harlem kitchen of the late "Queen of Soul Food", Sylvia Woods. Waffles with chicken are the star turn. Try and get a spot at the bar for the best experience. *Daily | 328 Malcolm X Blvd | tel. 1 212 9 96 06 60 | sylvias restaurant.com | Subway 2, 3 125th Street | Harlem | ▥ 0*

56 THAI DINER

For decades, gourmands have argued about which of New York's Thai restaurants is the best. *Uncle Boons* was always a contender, as was its off-shoot, *Uncle Boons Sister*. Now the owners have combined the best of each restaurant to create the menu at the Thai Diner and achieved another culinary hit! *Daily | 186 Mott Street | tel. 1 646 5 59 41 40 | thaidiner.com | Subway J, Z Bowery | Nolita | ▥ D15*

57 PANNA II

There are flashing lights in the ceiling of this neighbourhood Indian restaurant lending it an Instagrammable psychedelic vibe. The food is great and good value too. *Daily | 93 E 1st Av. | tel. 1 212 5 98 46 10 | panna2.com | Subway F 2nd Av. | East Village | ▥ E14*

58 NITEHAWK

INSIDER TIP
Food and a film

Dinner at the cinema? Top chef Saul Bolton has made this possible at his great restaurant-cum-movie house. As well as the original in Williamsburg, there is now another branch right on Prospect Park *(188 Prospect Park West | nitehawkcinema.com/prospectpark).*

Daily | 136 Metropolitan Av. | tel. 1 646 9 63 92 88 | nitehawkcinema.com | Subway L Bedford Av. | Williamsburg | ▥ J15

59 L&B SPUMONI GARDENS

This excellent beer garden deep in Brooklyn is free of the hordes of tourists in other places. A huge piece of pizza costs less than $3 and there is spumoni ice cream for pudding – a proper Brooklyn experience. *Daily | 2725 86th Street | Tel. 1 718 4 49 12 30 | spumonigardens.com | Subway N, Q, W Av. U | Gravesend | ▥ 0*

60 VANESSA'S DUMPLING HOUSE 🐖

Eight fried Chinese dumplings with

Authentic, delicious, affordable: Vanessa's Dumpling House

a pork filling for $5.50, sesame pancakes with pork $4.50 – can it get any cheaper and still taste as great? *Daily | Several branches, incl. 118A Eldridge Street | tel. 1 212 6 25 80 08 | vanessas.com | Subway B, D Grand Street | Chinatown | ⌑ D–E15*

61 ALPHA DONUTS

A truly wonderful old diner in Queens which serves eggs, sandwiches, burgers and donuts. *Daily | 45–16 Queens Blvd | tel. 1 718 4 72 47 25 | Subway 7 46th Street-Bliss Street | Sunnyside | ⌑ 0*

62 MAMA'S TOO!

This Upper West Side place may only serve simple slices of pizza, but they

are so good that even the food critics at the *New York Times* are die-hard fans. *Daily | 2750 Broadway | tel. 1 212 5 10 72 56 | mamastoo.com | Subway 1 103rd Street | Upper West Side | ⌑ 0*

63 GANESH TEMPLE CANTEEN 🍴

The cellar of this beautiful Hindu temple in Flushing is home to this canteen where anyone can come to eat. The menu is Indian, largely vegetarian and cheap (nothing costs more than $10). *Daily. | 143–09 Holly Av. | tel. 1 718 4 60 84 84 | canteen.nyganesh temple.org | Subway 7 Flushing-Main Street | Flushing | ⌑ 0*

64 ANITA

"La Mamma del Gelato" began her business in Israel but, luckily, you can also find her ice cream in New York. Try out a variety of flavours – there are vegan and sugar-free options too. *Daily | 1561 2nd Av./81st Street | tel. 1 646 8 61 19 57 | anita-gelato.com | Subway Q 86th Street | Upper East Side | ⌑ K4*

65 NEW FULTON FISH MARKET

You'd only get it fresher if you fished it yourself! The USA's biggest fish market has been selling high-quality fish since 1822. The market pretty much only sells to smart restaurants nowadays but **INSIDER TIP** nightowls are welcome **Night-fishing** to show up and haggle with the friendly stallholders from 2am. *Mon–Fri 2–7am | 800 Food Center Dr. | tel. 1 718 3 78 23 56 | newfultonfishmarket.com | Bus Bx6 | Bronx | ⌑ 0*

SHOPPING

The hottest trends, the classiest couture and the very best vintage – New York has it all. This metropolis is a shopper's paradise.

A day's shopping in New York can be an exhausting experience. Madison Avenue and Fifth Avenue are packed full of huge department stores and flagship stores for international brands. There are charming smaller shops in SoHo, Chelsea and the Lower East Side, as well as in Williamsburg, Cobble Hill and Carroll Gardens in Brooklyn.

You'll find all the venues in this chapter on the pull-out map

A touch of kitsch: Big Apple souvenirs

Many US chains are already present on high streets in Europe, and the exchange rate is no longer favourable for Brits in the US. However, the sheer quantity and variety of retail outlets make shopping in New York a unique experience. Most shops are open late into the evening and at the weekend – we've listed any unusual opening times in the text – so there should be hardly any barriers preventing you from finding that perfect souvenir. Watch out though: most labelled prices don't include tax!

WHERE NEW YORK SHOPS

MARCO POLO HIGHLIGHTS

★ **STRAND BOOK STORE**
New and good-value used books. A bibliophile's heaven ➤ p. 91

★ **BERGDORF GOODMAN**
Elegant department store with the best window displays in the city, especially in the run-up to Christmas ➤ p. 92

★ **MOMA DESIGN STORE**
The world's most famous art museum has two retail outlets: on 53rd Street and in the middle of SoHo. Both sell modern art and cool design pieces ➤ p. 95

★ **APPLE STORE**
The trendy electronics giant's NYC flagship store ➤ p. 95

CHELSEA & HERALD SQUARE

Macy's department store and Chelsea market are the top two shopping destinations here

SOHO

Stroll through the pretty streets to find MoMa's design store and dozens of designer boutiques

Secaucus
95
Tonnelle Avenue
John F. Kenne
NEW JERSEY
Park Avenue
Union City
495
1 9
Weehawken
Palisade Avenue
Hoboken
Washington
River
Newark Avenue
Jersey City
Marin Boulevard
78
Montgomery Street
Grand Street
9a
Church St
Liberty State Park
478

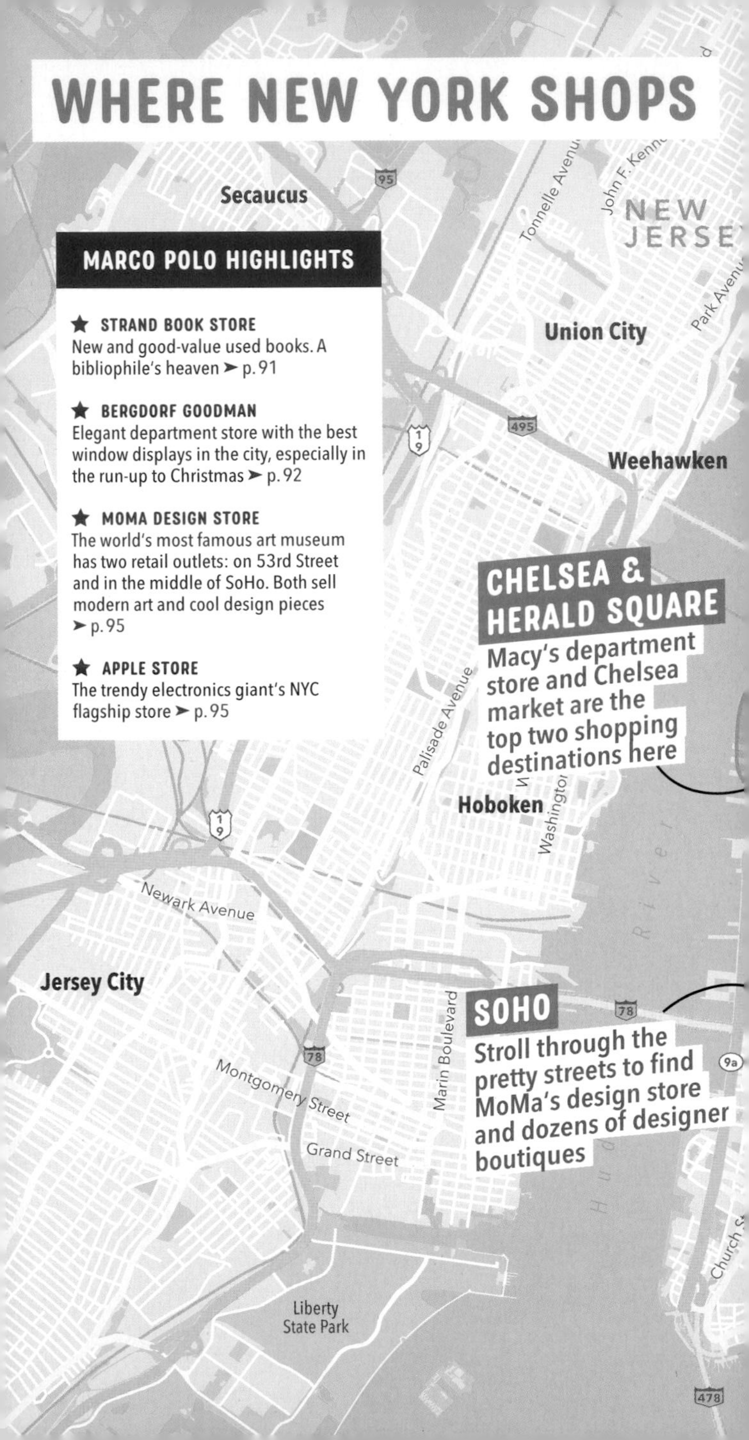

River Road

uttenberg

West 96th Street

NEW YORK

East 96th Street

278

West End Ave.

Amsterdam Avenue

Columbus Avenue

Central Park West

West 72nd Street

Madison Avenue

East 72nd Str.

York Aven

MADISON AVENUE
The world's longest
luxury shopping street

Central Park

Park Avenue

Broadway

10th Avenue

5th Avenue

Lexington Avenue

Broadway

21st Street

MANHATTAN

West 45th Street

Apple Store ★

Bergdorf Goodman ★ M 5th Avenue–59th Street

MoMA Design Store (53rd Street) ★

M 53rd Street–5th Avenue

5th Avenue M

East

FIFTH AVENUE
Shopping central: the
world's major chains
are all lined up for you

QUEENS

25

New York
Penn Station

M 28th Street

34th Str.

1st Avenue

Vernon Boulevard

495

18th Street

5th Avenue

Park Avenue South

FDR Drive

Franklin Street

WILLIAMSBURG
Stock up on vintage
finds in Brooklyn's
flea markets and
second-hand stores

Broadway-
M Lafayette Street

MoMA Design Store (Spring Street) ★

Avenue C

M

Nassau
Avenue

278

very M

Allen Street

Grand

Wythe Avenue

M Bedford Avenue

M Graham Avenue

LOWER EAST SIDE
Art galleries and
eccentric indie shops

Marcy Avenue M

Grand Str.

Bushwick Ave.

Lee Ave.

M Broadway

Broadway

78

BROOKLYN Flushing Avenue

M

Flushing
Avenue

1 km
0.62 mi

Strand Book Store ★

BOOKS

1 BARNES & NOBLE

A well-known chain with large shops across the city. Some New Yorkers while away an entire day here, so it's no surprise that these bookstores have become meeting places for (not so secret) literary trysts. *Lots of branches e.g. 33 E 17th Street | Subway L, N, Q, R, 4–6 14th Street-Union Square | Gramercy Park | ⌗ E12; 97 Warren Street/Greenwich Street | Subway 1, 2, 3 Chambers Street | Tribeca | ⌗ B16; barnesandnoble.com*

2 THE BGSQD BOOKSTORE

A lovely and well-curated bookshop with a focus on books for the LGBTQ community in the West Village. Its organise events, shows films and runs workshops (mostly with cheap beer and wine). *208 W 13th Street, Room 210, 2nd floor | bgsqd.com | Subway 1, 2, 3 14th Street | West Village | ⌗ C11*

WHERE TO START?

Where could be better than the world's largest department store – **Macy's** *(⌗ E9)*? This emporium takes up an entire block. And nearby on Herald Square, H&M and Gap have their flagship stores. For high-end boutiques head straight to **Madison Avenue** in Midtown and the Upper East Side *(⌗ G–H 6–7)*. And **Broadway** around Houston Street *(⌗ D14)* is the best spot in town for good-value clothes.

---

3 DASHWOOD BOOKS

Photographic books in all sizes … and prices! Go down the few steps to this magical bookshop, and you will be delighted by the small but exquisite range. *Tue–Sun from noon | 33 Bond Street | dashwoodbooks.com | Subway 6 Bleecker Street | NoHo | ⌗ D14*

4 THE LIT. BAR

When Noëlle Santos opened her LitBar in 2019, it was the only bookshop in the whole of the Bronx. But this place offers its community more than books: gifts, drinks and events are all on offer too. *Tue–Sun from noon | 131 Alexander Av. | thelitbar.com | Subway 4, 5 138th Street-Grand Concourse | Bronx | ⌗ 0*

5 POWERHOUSE ARENA

Great bookshop in Dumbo founded by a German. The shop belongs to a publishing house of the same name and it plays host to lots of events, parties and exhibitions. *28 Adams Street | powerhousearena.com | Subway F York Street, A, C High Street | Dumbo | ⌗ E18*

INSIDER TIP
Book parties

6 MOLASSES BOOKS 🐖

This cosy bookstore (owned by a small publisher of the same name) sells high-quality second-hand books. You can swap your own reading matter for something new or just sit down over a beer to read. Occasional DJ sets too. *7 Hart Street | Subway M Knickerbocker Av. | Bushwick | ⌗ 0*

Return to the analogue world: the Strand Book Store is a beacon in the digital age

7 STRAND BOOK STORE ★

A book-lover's dream! Some 18.5 miles of shelving stocked with new and used books as well as New York's largest selection of rare art and photography books for bibliophiles to explore. This family business was founded in 1927 and is the sole survivor of the original 47 book traders that started out on New York's famous Book Row. There's a branch on the Upper West Side too. *828 Broadway/ 12th Street | strandbooks.com | Subway L, N, Q, R, 4–6 14th Street-Union Square | East Village | E12*

DELIS & FINE FOOD

8 CHELSEA MARKET

Where the famous Oreo cookie was created is now home to stylish shops and gourmet restaurants selling all kinds of organic and fair-trade delights from across the world (inc. Italy, Japan, Thailand, Australia, Mexico and Morocco). The building, which once belonged to the National Biscuit Company, lends the market, including its gourmet stalls, the right kind of industrial charm. *75 9th Av./15th Street | Subway A, C, E 14th Street | Chelsea | B-C10–11*

9 LEVAIN BAKERY

People queue for hours for Levain's cookies and it is worth it too: whether you choose the walnut, chocolate-chip or peanut-butter varieties, these baked goods are a cut above your normal cookie. But be warned: they are not light bites! They were originally created as energy snacks to help the two bakers get through triathlons. The rest of the goodies on display are just as delicious. If the queue at the original bakery is too long, try one of the other branches, including on Amsterdam Avenue and in Harlem. *167 W 74th Street | levainbakery.com | Subway 1, 2, 3 72nd Street | Upper West Side | ⌁ F4*

INSIDER TIP
Avoid the queue

⑩ FONG ON

Paul Eng didn't want to take over his family's tofu business, founded in 1933; he preferred being a celebrity photographer in Moscow. But eventually the business drew him back to Chinatown, and now the city's top chefs buy their tofu from him. It's perfect as a sweet or savoury snack. *Tue–Sun 11am–7pm | 81 Division St | instagram.com/fongon1933 | Subway F East Broadway | Chinatown | ⌁ D16*

⑪ DI PALO

There are Italian delicacies everywhere you look in this delightful deli with prosciutto hams hanging from the ceiling and huge wheels of Parmesan displayed on the counter along with salami and mozzarella. A feast for the senses. *200 Grand Street | instagram.com/dipalofinefoods | Subway B, D, Grand Street 6 Spring Street | Little Italy | ⌁ D15*

INSIDER TIP
Ceiling storeroom

⑫ ZABAR'S

Meg Ryan and Tom Hanks shopped in this classic deli in the 1990s' rom-com *You've Got Mail*. Come for the paperthin smoked salmon and the legendary selection of cheeses. *2245 Broadway | zabars.com | Subway 1 79th St | Upper West Side | ⌁ F3*

⑬ SUNRISE MART

Here you'll find great snacks to keep you going and beautifully packaged confectionary for the perfect gift. New York's best Japanese food emporium! *4 Stuyvesant Street | Subway 6 Astor Place | East Village | ⌁ E13*

⑭ ECONOMY CANDY 🐖

Pear drops, lollies, toffee, gummy bears, are there any sweets these guys don't have? A family business which has been selling traditional sweets and innovative creations, including sugar-free candy for the calorie conscious, for over 100 years. People come here from all over the city. *108 Rivington Street | economycandy.com | Subway F Delancey Street | Lower East Side | ⌁ E15*

DEPARTMENT STORES

⑮ BERGDORF GOODMAN ★

Exclusive French, Italian and young American designers and the best cosmetics department in New York. The women's store on the other side of Fifth Avenue also has a restaurant. The best Christmas window decorations in Manhattan! *754 5th Av./ between 57th and 58th Street | bergdorfgoodman.com | Subway N, R 5th Av. | Midtown | ⌁ G7*

16 SAKS FIFTH AVENUE

You can buy anything and everything in the original flagship store of this famous chain. Look out for special offers and sales. And don't miss the musical window displays if you're here before Christmas. *611 5th Av./50th Street | saksfifthavenue.com | Subway E, M 5th Av.-53rd Street | Midtown | ⌶ G8*

17 BLOOMINGDALE'S

A high-class department store selling fashion by American designers and international labels. *1000 3rd Av./ between 59th and 60th Street | bloomingdales.com | Subway N, R, 4-6 Lexington Av./59th Street | Upper East Side | ⌶ H7*

18 MACY'S 🚩

One of the world's biggest department stores! Women can start their shopping spree with a make-up session downstairs before exploring its many floors. The store organises a huge Thanksgiving Parade with floats and plenty of balloons every year. *151 W 34th Street/Broadway | macys.com | Subway B, D, F, N, Q, R 34th Street-Herald Square | Midtown South | ⌶ E9*

Shopping galore at Macy's, the world's largest department store

MISCELLANEOUS

19 FLOWER DISTRICT

A whole block devoted to flowers and plants! Take a stroll through this oasis in the concrete jungle and come back 🚩 in the evenings when there are good deals. *28th Street/between 6th and 7th Av. | Subway N, Q, R, W 28 Street | Chelsea | ⌶ D–E10*

20 CELSIOUS

Two sisters from Germany have realised their dream of owning their own laundromat. Do your laundry, sip a cappuccino, catch-up on some work or shop for eco-friendly cleaning products – all in the same space. *115 N 7th Street | celsious.com | Subway L Bedford Av. | Williamsburg | ⌶ J15*

21 BEADS OF PARADISE

Smiling Buddhas in yellow, green and red; display cases bursting with jewellery, silk scarves and beads galore for creative buyers. Make a souvenir necklace all by yourself! *16 E 17th Street/5th Av. | beadsofparadisenyc.com | Subway L, N, Q, R, 4-6 14th Street-Union Square | Flatiron District | ⌶ D-E12*

22 PEARL RIVER MART

A huge gift shop on Broadway selling huge quantities of cheap goodies. Cool, colourful and creative. *452 Broadway | pearlriver.com | Subway N, Q, R, W Canal Street | Tribeca | ▥ C15*

23 CONTAINER STORE

Ever worried about not having enough storage? This shop has every conceivable type of box for kitchens, offices and garages. Travel accessories and eccentric gifts too. *629 6th Av. | containerstore.com | Subway F, M 23 Street | Flatiron District | ▥ D11*

24 FISH'S EDDY

From mugs with New York scenes and plates depicting the city's skyline to T-shirts made from organic cotton. Ideal for souvenirs. *889 Broadway/ 19th Street | fishseddy.com | Subway R, 6 23 Street | Flatiron District | ▥ E11*

25 HAMMACHER SCHLEMMER

An eclectic mix of gifts ranging from hi-tech, futuristic noise cancellers to trad, comfy PJs. *Closed Sun | 147 E 57th Street/near Lexington Av. | hammacher.com | Subway N, R, 4–6 Lexington Av./59th Street | Midtown East | ▥ H7*

26 LOVE, ADORNED

Charming shop for jewellery, accessories and home deco in SoHo. *269 Elizabeth Street/E Houston Street | loveadorned.com | Subway F 2nd Av. | SoHo | ▥ D14*

27 MAKARI

Beautiful Japanese art, crafts and tiny antiques: a bit of Tokyo at the heart of the East Village. Quiet, elegant and not easy on the wallet – but it costs nothing to look around. *97 3rd Av./ near 12th Street | themakari.com | Subway L 3rd Av. | East Village | ▥ E12*

Worshipping at the shrine: disciples of technology outside New York's Apple Store

28 MOMA DESIGN STORE ★

A great interior décor selection and a whole range of items for everyday use from the collection of the Museum of Modern Art. *Branches at 11 W 53rd Street, between 5th and 6th Av. | Subway B, D, F, M 47–50th Street | Midtown | ⌖ G7; 81 Spring Street at Crosby Street | Subway 6 Spring Street | SoHo | ⌖ D14; momastore.org*

29 MUJI

Waterproof speakers, New York skyscrapers made from wooden blocks, unusual fashion – a wide variety of interesting household novelties. Four branches including *455 Broadway | muji.us | Subway N, Q, 6 Canal Street | SoHo | ⌖ C15*

30 WING ON WO & CO.

**INSIDER TIP
Pretty
porcelain**

The oldest shop in Chinatown (founded in 1925!) is charming and sells antique porcelain figures, glazed bowls, colourful cups and tea sets. Three generations of a Chinese family have run this store. *26 Mott Street | wingonwoand.co | Subway J, Z Chambers Street | Chinatown | ⌖ C16*

31 CITYSTORE

Socks with the subway on them, fire service calendars, toy taxis and Manhattan magnets. Owned by the city, this shop sells everything a NYC junkie could ever desire … and more. *1 Centre Street | a856-citystore.nyc.gov | Subway 4, 5, 6, J, M Brooklyn Bridge | Civic Center | ⌖ C16*

ELECTRONICS

32 APPLE STORE ★

Whether it's the MacBook, the iPhone, the iPad or AirPods – Apple still decides what is cool. Workshops run by experts are held daily on software and hardware. Open 24/7. *767 5th Av./59th Street | apple.com/retail/fifthavenue | Subway 4–6 59th Street, F 57th Street | Midtown East | ⌖ G7*

33 B&H PHOTO 🐖

A huge emporium for photography and film. You can rent things too. *Closed Sat | 420 9th Av./33rd Street | bhphotovideo.com | Subway A, C, E 34th Street | Garment District | ⌖ D9*

34 NINTENDO NY 👾

Thousands of consoles and games just waiting to be tested out. *10 Rockefeller Plaza/48th Street, 5th Av. | nintendo worldstore.com | Subway N, Q, R, S, 1, 2, 3, 7 Times Sq-42nd Street | Diamond District | ⌖ F8*

FLEA MARKETS

35 GRAND BAZAAR NYC

Shoppers at the city's largest weekly flea market can spend to their heart's content, and a large proportion of the proceeds from the market go to local public schools. Great food at the Farmers' Market next door. *100 W 77th Street | grandbazaarnyc.org | Subway B, C 81st Street | Upper West Side | ⌖ G3*

36 ARTISTS & FLEAS

Local artists, designers and artisans sell jewellery, clothes and much more at the weekend in a warehouse in Williamsburg *(70 North 7th Street/ between Kent and Wythe Av. | Subway L, Bedford Av. | Williamsburg | ⌑ J15)* and daily at *Chelsea Market (see p. 91) (88 10th Av./15th Street | Subway A, C, E, 14th Street | ⌑ B11). artistsandfleas.com*

GALLERIES

37 DAVID ZWIRNER
One of the most important galleries in the city showing innovative art in elegant surroundings on 20th Street. *537 W 20th Street/between 10th and 11th Av. | davidzwirner.com | Subway C, E 23rd Street | Chelsea | ⌑ B10*

38 MMUSEUMM
Is it a mini-museum? A gallery? Or "a place to look and think or look and not think," as it claims? Most likely, it's a fascinating mixture of all three, hidden away in a back alley. *4 Cortlandt Alley | mmuseumm.com | Subway 6 Canal Street | Tribeca | ⌑ C15*

39 GAGOSIAN
Larry Gagosian has built a small art empire for himself in New York. The exhibition spaces always host high-calibre art shows. Several locations, including *980 Madison Av. | gagosian.com | Subway 4, 6 77th Street | Upper Eastside | ⌑ H4*

SHOPS FOR CHILDREN

40 FAO SCHWARZ
It's back! In 2015 this legendary toy-shop was forced to close due to rising rents, but a new owner came in and was able to relaunch the shop in the Rockefeller Center. The oversized floor piano, which you play by dancing across the keys (as demonstrated by Tom Hanks in the 1988 film *Big*), is back too! *30 Rockefeller Plaza | faoschwarz.com | Subway B, D, F 47th–50th Streets Rockefeller Center | Diamond District | ⌑ F7*

41 DYLAN'S CANDY BAR
Sweets of all shapes, colours and flavours can be found in this candy emporium. *20 Hudson Yards | tel. 1 646 7 35 00 78 | dylanscandybar.com | Subway 7 34th Street-Hudson Yards | Hudson Yards | ⌑ C8*

42 LEGO STORE 👯
The huge Lego Store is a paradise for kids to play with building blocks – and then to make their parents buy them afterwards. *200 5th Av./23rd Street | stores.lego.com | Subway L, N, Q, R, 4 5, 6, 14th Street-Union Square | Flat Iron District | ⌑ E11*

43 LULU'S CUTS & TOYS
It's a lively place, this colourful toy-shop and hairdresser in Brooklyn's Park Slope. Every child can choose a video to watch while having a haircut and lots of toys make the wait a fun time. *| 48 5th Av. | tel. 1 718 8 32 37 32 | luluskidscuts.nyc | Subway 2, 3 4, 5 Atlantic Av./ Barclays Center | Brooklyn | ⌑ L23*

44 GAP
One of Gap's many Manhattan stores includes Baby Gap (ages newborn to

five years) and Gap Kids ranges. *1988 Broadway | gap.com | Subway 1 66th Street-Lincoln Center | Upper West Side | ⊞ F4*

45 GRANDMA'S PLACE
A former school teacher and real-life grandma runs this cute shop in Harlem. When it comes to toys, she knows her stuff! *84 W 120th Street | grandmasplaceinharlem.com | Subway 2,3 116th Street | Harlem | ⊞ 0*

46 MARY ARNOLD TOYS
The USA's oldest toyshop had to move after its rent was raised but remains a paradise for children. Everything from dolls and clothes for babies to teenage-friendly toys. *1178 Lexington Av. | maryarnoldtoys.com | Subway 6 77th Street | Upper East Side | ⊞ J4*

FASHION & ACCESSORIES

47 DESIGNER SHOE WAREHOUSE 🐾
Cool shoes for a good price? This shop has more shoes than anyone could ever wear in their life. Several branches, including *40 E 14th Street | dsw.com | Subway L, N, Q, R, 4, 5, 6 14th Street-Union Square | Union Square | ⊞ E12*

48 AEROPOSTALE
A chain that sells hip clothing at unbeatable prices. Young, fresh and cheeky fashion for girls 'n' guys. Lots of special deals. *100 W 33rd Street | aeropostale.com | Subway B, D, F, M, N, Q, R 34th Street | Herald Square | ⊞ E9*

A military encounter in the Lego Store

49 BEACON'S CLOSET
Four women from Brooklyn got their heads together, and the result was this chain of cool stores selling vintage clothes. Classic designs, off-the-wall cool and a huge selection! Four branches, including *10 W 13th Street | Subway F, M 14th Street | Greenwich Village | ⊞ E12; 74 Guernsey Street | Subway G Nassau Av. | Greenpoint | ⊞ K14; beaconscloset. com*

INSIDER TIP
Vintage, creative, cool and crazy

50 FLIGHT CLUB
Buying sneakers can be something of a sport for New Yorkers. People will queue for hours or go on wild goose chases across the city to try and get ahead of the game. This decade-old

Shopping or science fiction? The futuristic Hudson Yards

shop is one of the few where you can find very cool trainers in a normal way. The staff are specialists and sell a range of shoes, from collectors' items kept in glass cases and sold for astronomical prices to everyday trainers sold at everyday prices – truly something for everyone. *812 Broadway | flightclub.com | Subway L, N, Q, R, 4, 5, 6 14th Street-Union Square | Greenwich Village | ⮞ E12*

51 CENTURY 21

In the 1990s, Carrie from *Sex and the City* browsed through the huge selection of discounted designer clothes and accessories in this shop while chatting to Mr Big on the phone. The chain went bankrupt during the pandemic and was sorely missed by New Yorkers. So fashionistas on a budget were delighted when the flagship store on Cortlandt Street reopened for business in spring 2023. *22 Cortlandt Street | c21stores.com | Subway A, C, J, Z, 2, 3, 4, 5 Fulton Street | Financial District | ⮞ B17*

52 J. CREW & MADEWELL

Colourful, young and hip: these two sister chains, which belong to the same parent company, offer fashion for the office and for the party, usually at affordable prices. There are numerous branches, including *230 Vesey Street | madewell.com | jcrew.com | Subway E World Trade Center | Battery Park City | ⮞ A16*

53 HOUSING WORKS 🛒

Excellent second-hand shops selling clothes, books and furniture. Housing Works collects money for HIV-positive homeless men, women and children, and its stores are stocked with high-quality objects generously donated by enthusiastic New Yorkers. *Lots of branches in Manhattan and Brooklyn, incl 130 Crosby Street | housingworks.com | Subway B, D, F Broadway-Lafayette Street | Nolita | ◫ D14*

54 TODD SNYDER AT THE LIQUOR STORE

Steve McQueen-style men's fashion by Todd Snyder housed in a former bar. *235 W Broadway | toddsnyder. com | Subway A, C, E 1 Canal Street | Tribeca | ◫ B15*

55 MARC JACOBS

Fashion and accessories by the crown prince of American fashion design. *127 Prince Street | marcjacobs.com | Subway N, R Prince Street | SoHo | ◫ C14*

56 PRADA

In addition to haute couture, this Prada store offers a uniquely 21st-century shopping experience – with AI-driven changing rooms. *575 Broadway/Prince Street | prada.com | Subway N, R Prince Street | SoHo | ◫ D14*

57 REI

This cooperative sells everything you need for walking, skiing, climbing, canoeing, jogging or cycling, from rucksacks to down jackets and ski suits. The staff give excellent advice, and the building in SoHo is one of the most attractive in the district. *303 Lafayette Street | rei.com | Subway B, D, F, M Broadway-Lafayette | SoHo | ◫ D14*

58 DOVER STREET MARKET

The clothes on sale here are unusual and pricey, but don't let that put you off. Rei Kawakubo of Comme Des Garçons has turned this former design school into a shopping temple. Gawping at your surroundings

INSIDER TIP
No need to shop – just look around

is all part of the fun. *Mon–Sat 11am–6pm, Sun noon–5pm | 160 Lexington Av. | newyork.doverstreet market.com | Subway 6 33rd Street | Murray Hill | ◫ F10*

59 HUDSON YARDS

This relatively new district on the west side of Manhattan has a shopping mall with dozens of high-end shops that offer the latest and best in fashion, beauty, kids' stuff, jewellery and household goods. You could spend hours window-shopping here! *hudsonyardsnewyork.com | Subway 7 34th Street-Hudson Yards | Hudson Yards | ◫ C8*

60 VINTAGE THRIFT STOP

Wonderful small second-hand shop whose profits support a Jewish charity. The best objects are put in the window and auctioned off. There is a second branch in the West Village. *286 3rd Av. | vintagethriftshop.org | Subway 6 23rd Street | Gramercy | ◫ F11*

61 VIVIENNE WESTWOOD

Three floors of London plush-punk and hip new collections for men and women by the late, great fashion icon Vivienne Westwood. How about a heart-shaped black leather bag? Yours for $400! *14 E 55 Street | vivienne westwood.com | Subway E, M 5th Av./53rd Street | Midtown East |* 🔲 *G7*

62 SAMPLE SALES 🐷

Reduced designer fashions, cut-price display items and lots of other discounts – New Yorkers love sample sales! They are generally organised at short notice and in new locales; for up-to-date information, check online at *thestylishcity.com*.

HAIR & BEAUTY

63 AVEDA INSTITUTE

This beauty salon is ideal for a quick treatment in the middle of a shopping trip. The institute is also a school, and 🐷 if you let trainees do your facial or colour, you'll be charged half price (they also tend to be twice as careful!)

233 Spring Street/between 6th A *and Varick Street | tel. 1 212 807 14 92* *| avedaarts.edu/locations/new-york* *Subway 1 Houston Street | SoHo* 🔲 *C14*

64 FRÉDÉRIC FEKKAI

Stylist to the stars, Fekkai counts celebrities such as Liv Tyler and Naomi Watts among his clients. Today, he charges $750 for a haircut. Cuts by the salon's other stylists are reasonable by comparison at $165. *394 W Broadway | tel. 1 212 8 88 26 00* *fekkai.com | Subway A, C, E Spring Street | SoHo |* 🔲 *C14*

65 DRAMATICS NYC

This chain does good-value haircuts No need to make an appointment; just pop in and wait your turn. The staff are skilful and friendly, and

Breakfast at Tiffany's? It's served on the fourth floor at this famous jeweller

they charge substantially less than $50 per cut. Lots of branches, incl. *2468 Broadway | dramaticsnyc.com | Subway 1, 2, 3 96th Street | Upper West Side | ▥ G1*

66 KIEHL'S PHARMACY

An old-fashioned pharmacy that's famous for its own skin and hair-care lines. No animal testing. Lots of outlets, the most beautiful is *109 3rd Av./between 13th and 14th Street | kiehls.com | Subway L, N, Q, R, 4–6 14th Street-Union Square | East Village | ▥ E12*

67 SEPHORA

This is where New Yorkers head for their cosmetics and beauty tips. Numerous branches, including *557 Broadway/between Spring and Prince Streets | sephora.com | Subway N, R Prince Street SoHo | ▥ D14*

MUSIC

68 ACADEMY RECORDS

Vinyl is alive and kicking! This impressive record store in Greenpoint has more than 100,000 new and second-hand vinyls in stock, as well as CDs. *85 Oak Street/between West and Franklin Street | academy-lps.com | Subway G Greenpoint Av. | Greenpoint | ▥ J13*

69 JAZZ RECORD CENTER

The name says it all – jazz is what this store is all about. *Closed Sun | 236 W 26th Street/between 7th and 8th Av., 8th floor | jazzrecordcenter.com | Subway 1 28th Street | Chelsea | ▥ D10*

OUTLET STORE

70 WOODBURY COMMON PREMIUM OUTLETS

Located outside the city, Woodbury Common is a popular destination thanks to its 220 outlet stores from world-famous high-end brands, including Prada, Miu Miu, Marc Jacobs, Armani and Gucci. *Travel tickets (incl. discount vouchers) are available from several bus companies: freetoursby-foot.com/woodbury-commons-bus | premiumoutlets.com/outlet/woodbury-common | ▥ 0*

JEWELLERY

71 TIFFANY & CO.

The recently renovated legendary jewellery store has prices that are equally legendary! Head to the third floor for (more) affordable silver knick-knacks. Breakfast is served on the fourth floor in a nod to the classic film; it may not be cheap, but in this part of town, it's a relative bargain! *727 5th Av./57th Street | tiffany.com | Subway B, C 57th Street | Midtown | ▥ G7*

72 DIAMOND DISTRICT

A whole block full of diamonds. Jewellers are lined up in a long row, which makes window-shopping all the more fun. *47th Street/between 5th and 6th Av. | Subway B, D, F 47th–50th Streets-Rockefeller Center | Diamond District | ▥ F8*

NIGHTLIFE

New Yorkers have more options for a night out than almost any other city dwellers around the globe, with plays, musicals, opera, jazz performances, classical concerts, bars, clubs and much more.

After work, lots of people go straight to their favourite bar for a drink or head to a restaurant to meet friends for an early dinner. Afterwards they head to the theatre or to the movies, before ending the evening at a trendy club. It can all be a bit overwhelming, so

You'll find all the venues in this chapter on the pull-out map

A little black dress is essential for New York nightlife: glamour at 230 Fifth

sometimes your best bet is to just spend an evening wandering around one part of town. No matter where you end up, it will be fun and lively.

Live music – especially jazz, blues and rock – is a speciality here; places like Williamsburg and Bushwick in Brooklyn attract a young crowd of enthusiastic revellers with their good prices, hip venues and cool music.

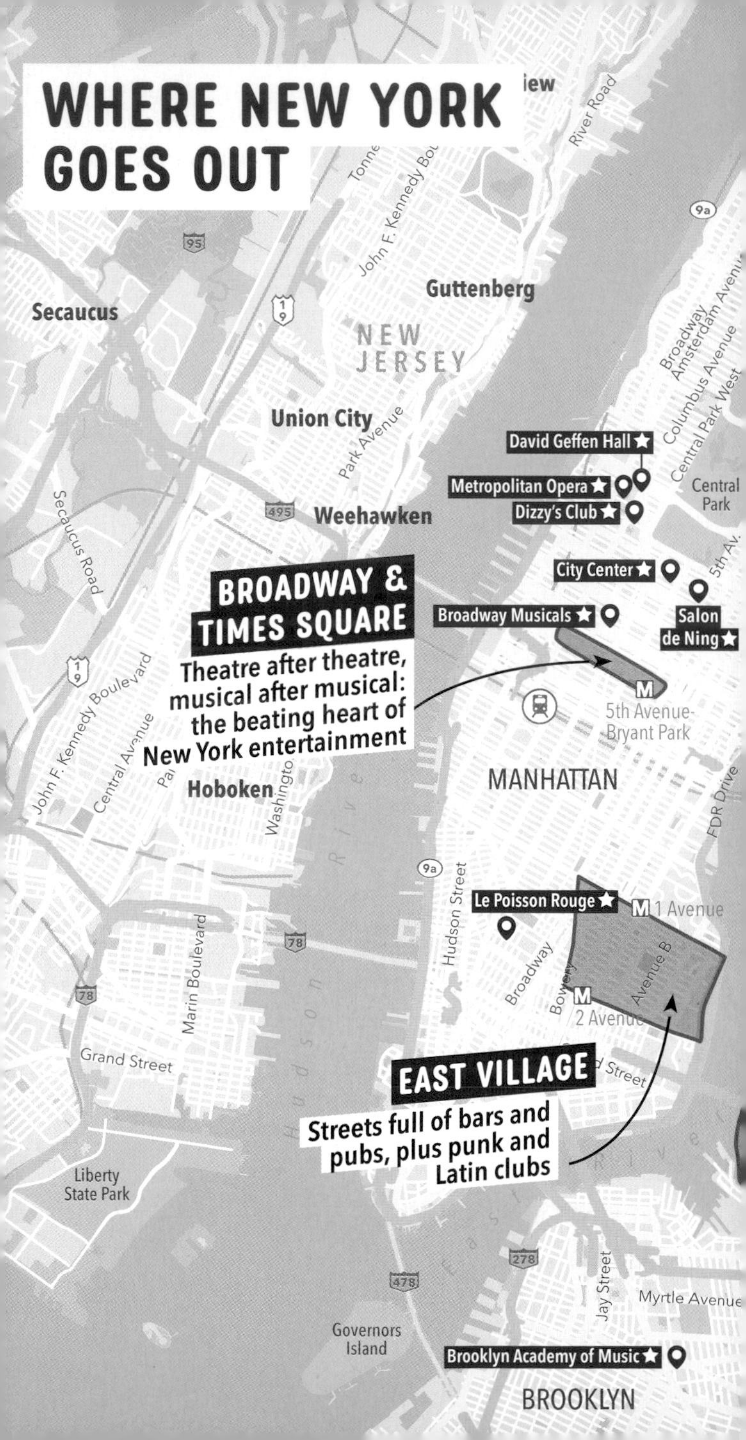

WHERE NEW YORK GOES OUT

Tonne
iew
River Road
John F. Kennedy Bou
9a

Secaucus

9
19

Guttenberg

NEW
JERSEY

Union City

Broadway
Amsterdam Avenue
Columbus Avenue
Central Park West

Park Avenue

95

495

Weehawken

David Geffen Hall ★

Metropolitan Opera ★

Dizzy's Club ★

Central Park

5th Av.

City Center ★

Broadway Musicals ★

Salon de Ning ★

BROADWAY & TIMES SQUARE

Theatre after theatre, musical after musical: the beating heart of New York entertainment

M 5th Avenue-Bryant Park

MANHATTAN

FDR Drive

Seacucus Road

John F. Kennedy Boulevard

Central Avenue

Washingto

Pa

Hoboken

19

9a

Hudson Street

Le Poisson Rouge ★

M 1 Avenue

Broadway

Bowery

Avenue B

Marin Boulevard

78

78

Hudson Rive

M 2 Avenue

Street

EAST VILLAGE

Streets full of bars and pubs, plus punk and Latin clubs

Grand Street

Liberty State Park

East River

Governors Island

278

478

Jay Street

Myrtle Avenue

Brooklyn Academy of Music ★

BROOKLYN

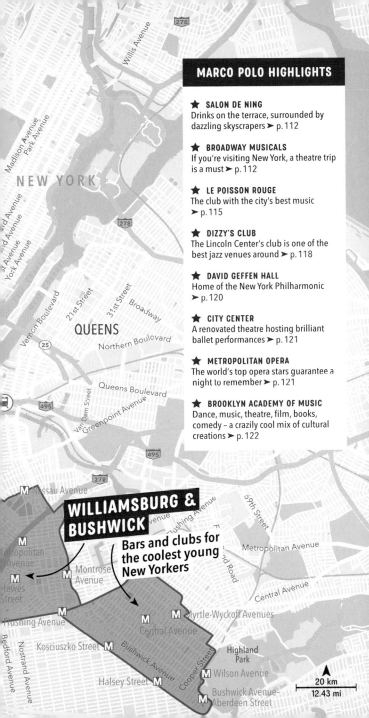

MARCO POLO HIGHLIGHTS

★ **SALON DE NING**
Drinks on the terrace, surrounded by dazzling skyscrapers ➤ p. 112

★ **BROADWAY MUSICALS**
If you're visiting New York, a theatre trip is a must ➤ p. 112

★ **LE POISSON ROUGE**
The club with the city's best music ➤ p. 115

★ **DIZZY'S CLUB**
The Lincoln Center's club is one of the best jazz venues around ➤ p. 118

★ **DAVID GEFFEN HALL**
Home of the New York Philharmonic ➤ p. 120

★ **CITY CENTER**
A renovated theatre hosting brilliant ballet performances ➤ p. 121

★ **METROPOLITAN OPERA**
The world's top opera stars guarantee a night to remember ➤ p. 121

★ **BROOKLYN ACADEMY OF MUSIC**
Dance, music, theatre, film, books, comedy – a crazily cool mix of cultural creations ➤ p. 122

WILLIAMSBURG & BUSHWICK

Bars and clubs for the coolest young New Yorkers

20 km
12.43 mi

BARS

Many of the best bars in the world are in the Big Apple. Hotel bars can be a good choice for sipping classic cocktails into the small hours alongside hotel guests and other bar flies. Particularly recommended are the *King Cole Bar* in *The St Regis, Le Bain* in the *Standard* and the Grand Bar in the *Hotel Soho Grand*.

Mixologists here love experimenting and are always on the lookout for cool new drinks. One recent trend has been to revive cocktails from the 17th and 18th centuries. These include the "Bishop", a kind of mulled wine, the "Flip" (high-proof alcohol with egg and sugar) and the "Cobbler" (wine, fruit and sugar).

When going out in NYC, remember to take some ID. You will be asked for it automatically in many places, even if you are clearly over the legal drinking age of 21.

WHERE TO START?

New York's nightlife is as varied as the city itself. A musical in the Theater District? Jazz in Greenwich Village? Or one of the many smaller bars and live music clubs on the Lower East Side? It's up to you. However you choose to spend you time, there's no better way to kick off your evening than at *Salon de Ning* (⚏ *G7*) on the rooftop of The Peninsula hotel. From here the city sparkles seductively, luring you into the night..

1 230 FIFTH

This large, award-winning roof terrace bar on Fifth Avenue lies in the middle of Midtown's sea of lights. When it gets colder, they provide blankets, and when it gets really cold, small igloos serve as cosy shelters. *230 5th Av./27th Street | tel. 1 212 7 25 43 00 | 230-fifth.com | subway: N, R, 6 28th Street| NoMad | ⚏ E10*

2 BEAUTY BAR

Could there be anything better than holding a Martini in your right hand while a professional paints the nails of your left? And then switches round! This bar-cum-beauty salon allows you to achieve this dream. *231 E 14th Street | tel. 1 212 5 39 13 89 | thebeautybar.com | Subway L 3rd Av. | Gramercy Park | ⚏ E12*

3 ALPHABET CITY BEER CO.

In the hip East Village, locals recline on a leather sofa to drink one of over 350 kinds of beer. *96th Av./near 7th Street | tel. 1 646 4 22 71 03 | abcbeer.co | Subway F 2nd Av. | East Village | ⚏ F14*

4 FLOYD

In this cosy, old-fashioned bar in Brooklyn Heights you can play petanque while you sip your beer. *131 Atlantic Av. | tel. 1 718 858 5810 | floydny.com | Subway 2, 3, 4, 5 Borough Hall | Brooklyn Heights | ⚏ H21*

5 APOTHÉKE

Barmen wearing white pharmacists' coats set light to absinthe, the green

Balthazar – for a taste of France in the middle of New York

MARKER TIP
What the doctor ordered

spirit that was prohibited for many years but is now very much "in". The bar is packed every evening. *9 Doyers Street/between Bowery and Pell Street | tel. 1 12 4 06 04 00 | apothekenyc. com | Subway N, Q, 6 Canal Street | Chinatown | ⫿ D16*

⑥ HOLLAND BAR

Loud music, cheap beer and eccentric drinkers. This is a classic dive bar – the perfect place for a fun evening! *532 9th Av. | Tel. 1 212 502 4609 | Subway A, C, E 42nd Street-Port Authority | Hudson Yards | ⫿ D8*

⑦ BALTHAZAR

This French brasserie is trendy without being snobby and serves a very decent steak frites. You can also just

order drinks at the bar and look out for celebrities. *80 Spring Street/Crosby Street | tel. 1 212 9 65 14 14 | balthazarny.com | Subway 6 Spring Street | Little Italy | ⫿ D14*

⑧ JIMMY'S CORNER

Finding a good bar with affordable drinks near Times Square is a real challenge – luckily, Jimmy's is here to save the day! There are photos all over the walls charting the life and career of the late landlord, who once trained Muhammad Ali. The beer is good value. *140 W 44th Street | tel. 1 212 2 21 95 10 | Subway 1, 2, 3, 7, N, Q, R, S Times Square-42nd Street | Theater District | ⫿ E8*

⑨ BARCADE

These bars are styled as game arcades. Grab yourself a freshly poured beer

Memorabilia for children's author Ludwig Bemelman, in the bar named after him

INSIDER TIP
Back to the eighties

and indulge in some retro fun, playing classic video games from the 1980s for 25 cents. Three branches: *148 W 24th Street | barcadenewyork.com | Subway 1, 23rd Street | Chelsea | ◫ D10; 6 St Marks Pl. | barcadestmarks.com | Subway 6 Astor Place | East Village | ◫ E13; 388 Union Av. | barcadebrooklyn.com | Subway L Lorimer Street | Brooklyn | ◫ K16*

⑩ LOCAL 138 🐷

A warm and welcoming neighbourhood pub with a very long happy hour. *181 Orchard Street | tel. 1 212 4 77 02 80 | Subway F Delancey Street | Lower East Side | ◫ E14*

⑪ SUNNY'S BAR

You'll feel immediately at home in this old-fashioned, friendly boozer on the harbour in Red Hook. *253 Conover Street | sunnysredhook.com | Bus B61, Beard Street/Van Brunt Street | Red Hook | ◫ E24*

⑫ BATHTUB GIN

The name alludes to the illicit gin that was made in bathtubs during the Prohibition. This charming place also serves cocktails and snacks. *132 9th Av./between 18th and 19th Streets | tel. 1 646 5 59 16 71 | bathtubginnyc.com | Subway A, C, E 14th Street | Chelsea | ◫ C10*

⑬ NOWHERE

Pleasant LGBTQ bar with daily deals on drinks, and a pool table. *322 E 14th Street | tel. 1 917 4 09 14 42 | nowhere barnyc.com | Subway L 1st Av. | East Village | ◫ E12–13*

14 BEMELMAN'S BAR

The stylish interior of this pretty piano bar in the Carlyle Hotel attracts an elegant clientele. *35 E 76th Street/ Madison Av. | tel. 1 212 7 44 16 00 | Subway 6 77th Street | Upper East Side | ⊞ H5*

15 THE BLIND BARBER

INSIDER TIP
Cocktail with your cut

Have your hair cut in this old-school barber shop and enjoy a cocktail, included in the price. *339 E 10th Street | tel. 1 212 228 21 23 | blindbarber.com | Subway L 1st Av. | East Village | ⊞ F13*

16 BRASS MONKEY

This bar has a relaxed atmosphere unlike most of the crowded places in the Meatpacking District. There's a view of the Hudson River from the rooftop terrace. *55 Little W 12th Street/ between Washington Street and 10th Av. | tel. 1 917 7 65 67 46 | brass monkeynyc.com | Subway A, C, E, 14th Street | Meatpacking District | ⊞ B11*

17 NEIR'S TAVERN

Do you enjoy the special atmosphere of a classic mafia movie? Then head straight to the Woodhaven District of Queens, where you'll find one of the oldest still-operating bars in the country. It's where many scenes from *Goodfellas* were shot. *87–48 78th Street | tel. 1 718 2 96 06 00 | neirs tavern.com | Subway J, 75th Street- Elderts Lane | Woodhaven | ⊞ 0*

18 BROADWAY DIVE

The locals all know each other at this bar, but they welcome newcomers into their midst. *2662 Broadway | tel. 1 212 8 65 26 62 | dive101.divebarnyc. com | Subway 1 103rd Street | Upper West Side | ⊞ 0*

19 CIBAR LOUNGE

Amazing Martini selection, which you can enjoy in front of an outdoor fire-place in a bamboo garden! *56 Irving Place between 17th and 18th Street | tel. 1 212 4 60 56 56 | cibarlounge. com | Subway N, Q, R, 4–6 14th Street- Union Square | Gramercy Park | ⊞ E12*

20 THE DEAD RABBIT GROCERY & GROG

This bar was named after an infamous 19th-century gang. Drinks are mixed on two floors; punch, bishops, flips and cobblers are all on offer. *30 Water Street | tel. 1 646 4 22 79 06 | dead rabbitnyc.com | subway: N, R Whitehall Street | Subway N, R Whitehall Street | Financial District | ⊞ B18*

21 THE DELANCEY

The roof not only has a bar, but also a garden with a fish pond and a dance club. Don't miss it! *168 Delancey Street | tel. 1 212 2 54 99 20 | the delancey.com | Subway F Delancey Street | Lower East Side | ⊞ E15*

22 THE FREEHOLD

This bar in Williamsburg feels like a hipster hotel; but instead of guest rooms, there are indoor and outdoor bars, ping-pong tables, WiFi and lots of regulars from the neighbourhood.

INSIDER TIP
Cocktails and ping-pong

45 S 3rd Street/near Wythe Av. | tel. 1 718 3 88 75 91 | freeholdbrooklyn. com | Subway J, M, Z Marcey Av. | Williamsburg | ⚇ H16

23 HENRY PUBLIC

This cosy and sophisticated bar looks like an elegant British pub from the 19th century. It serves classic long drinks, creative cocktails and delicious bites including an organic burger and a turkey sandwich that won an award from *New York Magazine*. 329 Henry Street/near Atlantic Av. | tel. 1 718 8 52 86 30 | henrypublic.com | Subway 2, 3, 4, 5 Borough Hall | Brooklyn | ⚇ H21

24 HOUSE OF WAX

More than 100 anatomical models, plus wax models of organs, surgical operations and abnormalities comprise the décor at this macabre joint. Sip on a Napoleon Death Mask and you'll blend right in! *445 Albee Square W | 1st floor | Brooklyn | tel. 1 718 5 13 25 47 | thehouseofwax. com | Subway 2, 3 Hoyt Street | Brooklyn | ⚇ K21*

25 EMPELLON AL PASTOR ROOFTOP & BAR

Olé! Enjoy spectacular views of the Empire State Building through the stone arches of this Spanish-style roof terrace. *145 E 39th Street | tel. 1 212 8 65 57 00 | empellon.com | Subway 4–7, S, Grand Central-42nd Street | Murray Hill | ⚇ G9*

26 MCSORLEY'S OLD ALE HOUSE

New York's oldest bar remained a

men-only space until 1970. The floor is covered in sawdust, and drinks are limited to a choice of light and dark beer, plus you have to order two at a time. Cheers! *15 E 7th Street/3rd Av. | tel. 1 212 473 91 48 | mcsorleysold alehouse.nyc | Subway 6 Astor Place | East Village | ⚇ E13*

27 EAR INN

Another old and comfortable joint, with good beer and burgers. Recently, it has added *Ear Out* for outside drinking. *326 Spring Street | tel. 1 212 2 26 90 60 | theearinn.com | Subway 1 Houston Street | West Village | ⚇ B14*

28 FANELLI'S CAFE

For decades, this place has been a

A warm summer evening up high on the terrace of the Press Lounge

meeting point for artists. Now surrounded by new luxury shops, it's one of the few original bars remaining from "old" SoHo. *94 Prince Street | tel. 1 212 226 94 12 | Subway R, W, N, Q Prince Street | SoHo | ⎕ C14*

29 PRESS LOUNGE

The rooftop, poolside bar at the Ink48 hotel has amazing views and plenty of space. *653 11th Av./48th Street | tel. 1 212 757 22 24 | ink48.com | Subway C, E, 1 50th Street | Hell's Kitchen | ⎕ D6*

30 DUTCH KILLS

Stunning cocktails with hand-cut ice in a classy old-fashioned setting. *27–24 Jackson Av. | tel. 1 718 3 83 27 24 |* *dutchkillsbar.com | Subway E, M, R Queens Plaza | Queens | ⎕ M10*

31 ROYAL PALMS SHUFFLEBOARD CLUB

Ever played shuffleboard? It's a game for two or four players that's a bit like curling.

INSIDER TIP
Brooklyn Shuffle

Give it a go in Brooklyn for \$40/hour. There's a bar for refreshments. *514 Union Street | tel. 1 347 2 23 44 10 | royalpalmsbrooklyn.com | Subway R Union Street | Brooklyn | ⎕ J23*

32 FLAGSHIP BREWERY

The motto is "unforgettable beer from the forgotten borough". Flagship has a cosy taproom next to its brewery on Staten Island. *40 Minthorne Street | tel. 1 718 6 91 59 07 | flagshipbrewery. nyc | Staten Island Ferry | Staten Island | ⌂ 0*

33 THE BRONX BREWERY

Beer is also being produced in the Bronx once again. Sample it in the brewery's pleasant bar/restaurant. *856 E 136th Street | tel. 1 718 4 02 10 00 | thebronxbrewery.com | Subway 6 Cypress Av. | Bronx | ⌂ 0*

34 RUDY'S BAR

The staff in this narrow bar run around with multiple pitchers of beer and plates of 🌭 free hot dogs as if they're in training for Munich's Oktoberfest. *627 9th Av./45th Street | tel. 1 646 7 07 08 90 | rudysbarnyc.com | Subway A, C, E 42nd Street-Port Authority Bus Terminal | Hell's Kitchen | ⌂ D7*

35 SALON DE NING ⭐

Check out this beautiful glass house on the 23rd floor of *The Peninsula* hotel. In the summer you can sit on the terrace between the skyscrapers and look out over the city. *700 5th Av./55th Street | tel. 1 212 9 03 39 95 | Subway E, M 5th Av. | Midtown | ⌂ G7*

36 SMITH & MILLS

This charming and offbeat pub is located in a restored coach house – it's a great place to enjoy some cocktails. *71 N Moore Street | tel. 1 646 8 58 14 33 | smithandmills.com | Subway 1 Franklin Street | Tribeca | ⌂ B15*

37 TØRST

A Danish bar with snacks, good beer and modern Scandi design. *615 Manhattan Av./between Driggs and Nassau Av. | tel. 1 718 3 89 60 34 | torstnyc.com | Subway G Nassau Av. | Greenpoint | ⌂ K14*

BROADWAY & MUSICALS

There are more than 40 theatres on Broadway which show a mixture of plays and ⭐ musicals. Hollywood stars often tread the boards here. Following the break enforced by the Covid pandemic, Broadway is booming once again.

The biggest hit of the last few years has been the hip-hop musical *Hamilton*, for which three-figure ticket prices are considered a bargain. But there's a huge choice of other shows on offer; you will have a great evening

no matter whether you see a Broadway stalwart, such as *Chicago*, *The Book of Mormon* or *Wicked*, or a family favourite, such as *Aladdin* or *The Lion King*.

Most theatres are closed on Mondays. There are often matinees on Wednesday, Saturday and Sunday afternoons. To see what is on, head online to *broadway.com*. Discounted tickets are available from TKTS ticket booths, among others *(tdf.org/nyc/7/TKTS-ticketbooths)*.

38 ELLEN'S STARDUST DINER 🚩

If you have not managed to get tickets for a Broadway show but still want to hear some classic musical numbers belted out live, then Ellen's Stardust Diner is here to help! The staff are mostly singers between jobs, and they will loudly serenade you while serving you your food. Great fun! *1650 Broadway | tel. 1 212 9 56 51 51 | ellensstardustdiner.com | Subway 1 50th Street | Midtown | ⌘ F7*

39 MARIE'S CRISIS CAFE

Prefer to sing yourself? The best place for that is this bar, which dates from the 1850s. Lots of Broadway professionals come here after a show to gather round

> **INSIDER TIP**
> Broadway karaoke

the piano and sing along in a big group. *59 Grove Street | tel. 1 646 4 70 60 40 | Subway A, B, C, D, E, F, M West 4th Street-Washington Square | Greenwich Village | ⌘ C12*

CLUBS & LIVE MUSIC

40 ARLENE'S GROCERY

A young audience and new bands. The musicians on stage change hourly generating plenty of noise, energy and enthusiasm. *Admission $5-10 |*

The famous sea of lights at the heart of the entertainment world: Broadway

95 Stanton Street/Orchard Street | tel. 1 212 358 16 33 | arlenesgrocery.net | Subway F 2nd Av. | *Lower East Side* | *E14–15*

41 BARBÈS 🐷

Great jazz, eastern European wind instruments, world music are all on the menu at this venue. The charming location, excellent live music, free entrance and an eclectic mix of patrons of all ages have elevated this small gem in Brooklyn to cult status. *376 9th Street/6th Av. | tel. 1 347 422 02 48 | barbesbrooklyn.com | Subway F, G 7th Av. | Brooklyn | K25*

42 THE BELL HOUSE 🐷

One of the best clubs in New York with live bands, DJs, table tennis competitions, bingo and TV-watch parties. Many events are free of charge; others cost $10 or more. *149 7th Street | tel. 1 718 643 65 10 | thebellhouseny. com | Subway F, G 9th Street-4th Av. | Brooklyn | J24*

43 BOWERY BALLROOM

Hip up-and-coming indie bands plus more established names, such as Patti Smith, grace this stage. *Admission $15–50 | 6 Delancey Street/between Bowery and Chrystie Streets | tel. 1 212 5 33 21 11 | boweryballroom. com | Subway F Delancey Street | Lower East Side | D15*

44 BOWERY ELECTRIC

This club on the Bowery hosts live rock concerts, with DJ sets on other nights. Two floors with three bars. *327 Bowery/2nd Street | tel. 1 212 2*

28 02 28 | *theboweryelectric.com | Subway 6 Bleecker Street | East Village | D14*

45 GONZALEZ Y GONZALEZ

This place serves Mexican food with a side order of dancing from Tuesday to Sunday. Salsa, meren-

INSIDER TIP
Dance the night away

gue and reggae rhythms ensure a memorable night out. *192 Mercer Street | tel. 1 212 4 73 87 87 | gygnyc. com | Subway 6 Bleecker Street | Greenwich Village | D14*

46 HOUSE OF YES

Have you ever done yoga to techno music? This is just one of the attractions at House of Yes in Bushwick. Acrobats float through the air, and there is burlesque dancing too. It all adds up to create one of New York's most colourful, crazy and unique nightlife venues, a mix of events space, restaurant, bar and garden. *Admission varies | 2 Wykoff Av. | Brooklyn | tel. 1 646 8 38 49 37 | houseofyes.org | Subway L Jefferson Street | Bushwick | 0*

INSIDER TIP
All in the m

47 MARQUEE

Funky house music, hip-hop or techno remixes to get you into the groove. *289 10th Av./26th Street | tel. 1 646 4 73 02 02 | marqueeny.com | Subway C, E 23rd Street | Chelsea | C9*

48 MERCURY LOUNGE 🐷

Very cool! Showcase for up-and-coming bands hoping to make it big. Cheap

Mexican food and hot dancing: Gonzalez y Gonzalez

tickets. You might just discover the next internet sensation. *Admission $10–15 | 217 E Houston Street/ Essex Street | tel. 1 212 2 60 47 00 | mercuryloungenyc.com | Subway F 2nd Av. | Lower Side | ⊞ E14*

concerts range from experimental and folk to classical and even opera. *158 Bleecker Street | tel. 1 212 5 05 34 74 | lepoissonrouge.com | Subway A–F, M W 4th Street | Greenwich Village | ⊞ C13*

49 PIANOS 🐖

Instead of buying concert tickets, go to this bar and use the cash to enjoy some drinks while listening to excellent live music for very little or no money. *158 Ludlow Street | tel. 212 5 05 37 33 | pianosnyc.com | Subway F 2 Av. | Lower Side | ⊞ E15*

50 LE POISSON ROUGE ★

A night club for the best in live music, from Lady Gaga to David Byrne. The

51 ROCKWOOD MUSIC HALL 🐖

Red velvet curtains enclose this glazed music bar where admission is usually free, the music is fantastic and the patrons are friendly. There are gigs every evening by upcoming bands: not too big otherwise there'd no space for the fans. *196 Allen Street/Houston Street | tel. 1 212 477 41 55 | rock woodmusichall.com | Subway F 2nd Av. | Lower Side | ⊞ E14*

> **INSIDER TIP**
> Small venue, big atmosphere

52 ROUGH TRADE

INSIDER TIP
Record store gigs

The Rough Trade label has a record shop in the Rockefeller Center which hosts live events – many of them free! *30 Rockefeller Plaza | tel. 1 212 6 64 11 10 | roughtrade.com | Subway B, D, F, M 47th–50th Street-Rockefeller Center | Midtown | ⌕ F8*

53 S.O.B.'S

The name is an abbreviation for "Sounds of Brazil", so if Caribbean and Brazilian music or salsa and reggae are your thing, this is the place for you. *Admission $10–40 | 204 Varick Street/ Houston Street | tel. 1 212 2 43 49 40 | sobs.com | Subway 1 Houston Street | SoHo | ⌕ C13*

54 UNION HALL

Something for everyone: downstairs, there's karaoke, comedy, live music and DJs; upstairs, play petanque, sit by the fireplace or browse in the house library. *702 Union Street/near 5th Av. | tel. 1 718 6 38 44 00 | union-hallnyc.com | Subway R Union Street | Brooklyn | ⌕ K24*

55 WARSAW CONCERTS

A hot spot for rock, indie and punk! *Admission varies | 261 Driggs Av./ Eckford Street | tel. 1 212 7 77 68 00 | FB: Warsaw Concerts | Subway L Lorimer Street | Brooklyn | ⌕ L14*

56 PETE'S CANDY STORE

Once a sweet shop, today this is a cool bar with live music and fair prices and occasional free readings, as well as performances on its small stage. *709 Lorimer Street | tel. 1 718 3 02 3. 70 | petescandystore.com | Subway . Lorimer Street | Williamsburg | ⌕ K15*

57 SOUL IN THE HORN

Hip-hop's home town has surprisingly few clubs dedicated to the genre. I you want to hear good hip-hop and rap, look out for special events. *Soul in the Horn (for dates and locations see soulinthehorn.com)* is a hugely popu lar series run by DJ Natasha Diggs incorporating live performances by legends and newcomers.

JAZZ & BLUES

58 ARTHUR'S TAVERN

Live jazz and blues every evening in this slightly old-fashioned nightclub in West Village. A good reason to visit

it's not as crowded as some of the better-known clubs. *57 Grove Street/near Seventh Av. | tel. 1 212 4 14 43 14 | arthurstavernnyc.com | Subway 1 Christopher Street | West Village | ⅏ C12*

🟥 BLUE NOTE

This famous club hosts the biggest names in the business. It may be crowded, and it's often expensive, but the music is brilliant. Reservation essential! *Admission $10–75 | 131 W 3rd Street/6th Av. | tel. 1 212 4 75 85 92 | bluenotejazz.com | Subway A–F, M West 4th Street | Greenwich Village | ⅏ C13*

🟥 BILL'S PLACE 🐷

If you want to listen to jazz in its Harlem birthplace, you can do a lot worse than Bill Saxton's place! This celebrated saxophonist performs with a small band at his home on Friday and Saturdays. With no more than about 30 guests, it is like a private concert and only costs $20. BYOB. *148 W 133rd Street | tel. 1 212 2 81 07 77 | billsplaceharlem.com | Subway 2,3 135th Street | Harlem | ⅏ 0*

🟥 NAMA

The New Amsterdam Musical Association is the oldest African-American music association in the country – it has retained many traditions throughout its 100-year-old history. The regulars all know each other, and they gather for a weekly music night every Monday – visitors welcome. *107 W 130th Street | tel. 1 212 2 81 13 50 | namaharlem.org | Subway 2,3 125th Street | Harlem | ⅏ 0*

A tropical feeling with music to match: it's the rhythm that matters at S.O.B's

62 DIZZY'S CLUB ⭐

The crème de la crème of jazz groove the night away in this club in the Lincoln Center. *Admission $10–150 plus $21 minimum spend| 33 W 60th Street/10 Columbus Circle | at Once Columbus Circle | tel. 1 212 2 58 95 95 | jazz.org/dizzys | Subway A–D, 1 59th Street-Columbus Circle | Columbus Circle | ▥ F6*

64 KNITTING FACTORY

You won't just hear avant-garde and traditional jazz at this legendary joint, but also alternative rock and pop, not to mention comedy evenings and brunch with drag queens. It also has multiple branches across the US and its own record label. *Admission $5–20 | 361 Metropolitan Av. | tel. 1 347 5 29 66 96 | bk.knittingfactory.com |*

Village Vanguard hits the high notes with jazz lovers

63 KNICKERBOCKER BAR & GRILL

Great atmosphere, world class jazz. Absolutely outstanding pianists and bass players perform in this wood-panelled bar with leather chairs. *Live music Fri, Sat from 9pm | admission $3.50 from 10.15pm | 33 University Place/9th Street | tel. 1 212 2 28 84 90 | knickerbockerbarandgrill.com | Subway 6 Astor Place | Greenwich Village | ▥ D12*

Subway L Bedford Av. | Brooklyn | ▥ K16

65 MINTON'S PLAYHOUSE

Greats like Charlie Parker, Thelonious Monk and Dizzy Gillespie all played in this venue – it's the ultimate New York jazz experience! *Live music Wed–Sun | 206 W 118 Street | tel. 1 212 8 66 12 62 | mintonsharlem.com | Subway B, C 116th Street | Harlem | ▥ 0*

66 PARLOR ENTERTAINMENT 🕊 🐷

Every Sunday at 4pm Marjorie Eliot, a jazz pianist and grande dame of the jazz scene, invites you into her lounge in Harlem for a jazz concert. This was once a well-kept secret, but it's now popular and the small apartment fills up quickly. *Admission free, voluntary donation | 555 Edgecombe Av./160th Street | Apt 3F | tel. 1 212 7 81 65 95 | Subway C 163rd Street | Washington Heights | ▥ 0*

67 SMALL'S

Who said cellars are for storage? Top-class jazz is played here in the basement until 4am –it's often packed, but always good! *Admission $25 | 183 W 10th Street/7th Av. | tel. 1 646 476 43 46 | smallslive.com | Subway 1 Christopher Street | West Village | ▥ C12*

68 VILLAGE VANGUARD

The most sought-after jazz club in town has top-class artists and the best acoustics. *Admission $30–40 plus one drink | 178 S 7th Av./11th Street | tel. 1 212 2 55 40 37 | villagevanguard.com | Subway 1–3 14th Street | Greenwich Village | ▥ C12*

CINEMA & FILM

69 ANGELIKA FILM CENTER

Cosy cinema with great films, loved by students, staff (and alumni) of New York University. *18 W Houston Street | tel. 1 212 9 95 25 70 | angelikafilmcenter.com | Subway B, D, F, M Broadway-Lafayette Street | NoHo | ▥ D14*

70 IFC CENTER

Art-house cinema with three screens in a former church in Greenwich Village. It belongs to AMC Networks who see it as a physical manifestation of their Independent Film Channel (IFC). The best of indie cinema! *323 6th Av. | ifccenter.com | Subway A, B, C, D, E, F, M West 4th Street/Washington Square | Greenwich Village | ▥ C13*

CONCERTS

The sheer number and range of concerts on any given evening in New York can be overwhelming and the quality is consistently high – as are the ticket prices. As a result, lots of classical music fans look forward to the summer when they can listen to free concerts in the open air with a picnic basket. The Philharmonic and the Metropolitan Opera are among those that lay on outdoor music performances, and they often throw in a firework display to complete the spectacle *(nyphil.org/parks)*!

INSIDER TIP Summer delight

Lincoln Center Plaza *(lincolncenter.org)* also hosts summer concerts, as does Central Park's *Summerstage (summerstage.org, p. 123)*.

71 BARCLAYS CENTER

Home to the Brooklyn Nets basketball team, this vast arena also hosts rock and pop concerts by the likes of Iron Maiden and Ed Sheeran, watched by up to 19,000 spectators. *620 Atlantic Av. | tel. 1 917 6 18 61 00 | barclayscenter.com | Subway B, D, N, Q, R, 2,*

A cathedral of culture: the world-famous Met in the Lincoln Center

3, 4, 5 Atlantic Av.-Barclays Center | Brooklyn | 📖 L23

72 BARGEMUSIC

A very special concert venue: enjoy chamber music on board a ship docked in Brooklyn with a great view of Manhattan (especially at night). *Thu–Sat 8pm, Sun 4pm | Fulton Ferry Landing | tickets $35–40, sometimes free | tel. 1 718 624 49 24 | barge music.org | Subway 2, 3 Clark Street | Brooklyn | 📖 D18*

73 CARNEGIE HALL

Allegedly, the violinist Jasha Heifetz was once been asked by a passer-by, "How do I get to Carnegie Hall?", to which he responded, "Practise!". Only the crème de la crème of soloists, orchestras and singers ever grace this stage. Its amazing acoustics mean it is often used for recordings. There are also backstage tours. *57th Street 7th Av. | tel. 1 212 247 78 00 carnegiehall.org | Subway N, R 57th Street | Midtown | 📖 F6*

74 DAVID GEFFEN HALL ★

This is the home of the world-famous New York Philharmonic orchestra. The entertainment tycoon, David Geffen donated $100 million to the hall's renovation to ensure it was named after him. *10 Lincoln Center/62nd Street | tel. 1 212 875 59 00 | nyphi org | Subway 1 66th Street | Lincoln Square | 📖 F5*

more competitive – the renowned *American Ballet Theatre* (ABT, *abt.org*) vies for prominence with the *New York City Ballet (nycballet.com)*, which is known for showcasing young talent.

76 CITY CENTER ⭐

The theatre aims to attract as broad an audience as possible to the performing arts. So its offering is wide, ranging from dance and musicals to drama. *131 W 55th Street/between 6th and 7th Av. | tel. 1 212 581 12 12 | nycitycenter.org | Subway N, R 57th Street | Midtown | ⫘ F7*

77 DAVID H. KOCH THEATER

This 1960s building by the prominent architect Philip Johnson is home to the city's two foremost ballet companies. *20 Lincoln Center/62nd Street | tel. 1 212 496 06 00 | davidhkoch theater.com | Subway 1 66th Street | Lincoln Square | ⫘ F5*

75 PARK AVENUE ARMORY

This arts centre in an iron structure dating from 1881 is impressively large and perfect for unusual performances, concerts and art exhibitions. It once even housed a fairground complete with Ferris wheel! *643 Park Av./ between 66th and 67th Street | tel. 1 212 616 39 30 | armoryonpark.org | Subway 4, 5, 6 68th Street | Lenox Hill | ⫘ H6*

78 THE JOYCE THEATER

The dance ensembles that perform on the stage here come from all over the world. *175 8th Av./19th Street | tel. 1 212 691 97 40 | joyce.org | Subway 1 18th Street | Chelsea | ⫘ C10*

OPERA & BALLET

York's largest opera house is the *Metropolitan Opera*. The Met is legendary and every singer in the world wants to sing on its stage in the Lincoln Center. The ballet scene is

79 METROPOLITAN OPERA ⭐

One of the most famous opera houses in the world, the Met was founded in 1883 by a group of millionaires. Every superstar in opera history has performed on the stage here. *30 Lincoln Center/62nd–66th Street | tel. 1 212 3 62 60 00 | met opera.org | Subway 1 66th Street | Lincoln Square | ⫘ E5*

Cradle of Black culture: remembering great stars at the Apollo Theater

80 NYU TISCH SCHOOL OF THE ARTS

The stars of tomorrow are trained for the spotlight here – the shows are great fun to watch. *111 2nd Av. | 3rd floor | tisch.nyu.edu/dance/second-avenue-dance-company | Subway F 2nd Av. | East Village | D13*

OFF-BROADWAY THEATRE & SHOWS

81 APOLLO THEATER

This theatre in Harlem, built in 1914, is one of the centres of African American culture in New York City.

INSIDER TIP
Harlem's got talent

It hosts concerts and events of all kinds. Every Wednesday there is a talent show for people with a thick skin. Musicians and dancers, comedians and rappers are judged by audience applause … or boos! Also recommended are the

behind-the-scenes tours with Billy Mitchell, who started work here more than 50 years ago as a runner and is now the in-house historian and is known as "Mr Apollo". *253 W 125th Street | tel. 1 212 5 31 53 00 | apollo theater.org | Subway 2, 3 125th Street | Harlem | 0*

82 BLUE MAN GROUP

The famous show has been taking the mickey out of the arts scene for nearly three decades. *Astor Place Theatre, 434 Lafayette Street | tel. 1 800 258 36 26 | blueman.com/new-york | Subway 6 Astor Place | NoHo | D13*

83 BROOKLYN ACADEMY OF MUSIC ★

Theatre and performing arts venue. Composer Philip Glass, theatre director Robert Wilson and musician and performing artist Laurie Anderson are among those who have staged pieces for this institution, which also has a cinema alongside its multiple live performance stages. *30 Lafayette Av./ between Felix Street and Ashland Place | Brooklyn | tel. 1 718 6 36 41 00 | bam.org | Subway 2–5, B, D, Q Atlantic Av.-Barclays Center | Brooklyn | ⌑ L22*

84 THE PUBLIC THEATER & JOE'S PUB

Contemporary theatre over several stages. If you prefer live music, *Joe's Pub (tel. 1 212 5 39 87 78 | joespub. com)* has played host to artists including Alicia Keys and Joss Stone. *425 Lafayette Street/Astor Place | tel. 1 212 5 39 85 00 | publictheater.org | Subway 6 Astor Place | Noho | ⌑ D13*

85 THE KITCHEN

Centre for music, performances, dance and video art, as well as literary events, discussions with artists and readings – serious, innovative, exciting. *512 W 19th Street/between 10th and 11th Av. | tel. 1 212 2 55 57 93 | the kitchen.org | Subway C, E 23rd Street | Chelsea | ⌑ B10*

86 NUYORICAN POETS CAFÉ

The large Puerto Rican community in New York has changed the city's cultural scene forever, thanks to the progressive writers who have given the US overseas territory a voice on the mainland. Two of them set up this café in the 1970s; it runs regular Nuyorican spoken word and poetry events. *236 E 3rd Street | tel. 1 212 7 80 93 86 | nuyorican.org | Subway J, M, Z Essex Street | Lower East Side | ⌑ F14*

87 CENTRAL PARK SUMMER STAGE

In July and August, Summer Stage is a series of free open-air concerts in Central Park. *Rumsey Playfield, above 72nd Street | summerstage.org | Subway 6 68th Street-Hunter College | Central Park | ⌑ H5*

88 COMEDY CELLAR

This is the most famous of the city's numerous high-quality comedy clubs. Many comedians performed here before they became household names. If you're lucky, they may stop by for quick show while you're there. *117 MacDougal Street | tel. 1 212 254 34 80 | comedycellar.com | Subway A, B, C, D, E, F, M W 4th Street-Washington Square | Greenwich Village | ⌑ C13*

89 LATE NIGHT TALK SHOWS ⚑

In theory, free tickets are available to the many late-night TV talk shows that are recorded in the city. However, they are extremely popular and so difficult to get hold of. For *Saturday Night Live*, for example, you have to send an email to snltickets@nbcuni. com in August and keep your fingers crossed. For *The Tonight Show* with *Jimmy Fallon (short.travel/new14)* you can try your luck online or in person at 9am at the entrance to the Rockefeller Center (49th Street), where standby tickets are given out. If you really want to see a show, you are best off looking for the slightly less famous ones. *Late Night with Seth Meyers (short.travel/new15)*, for example, often has tickets online.

ACTIVE & RELAXED

Watching the sunset: Brooklyn Bridge Park

SPORT & WELLNESS

BIRD WATCHING
Birding Bob (birdingbob.com) offers bird-watching walks around Central Park – or as he describes them: "Comedy shows with a little bit of bird watching" – for $10 per person.

JOGGING
The classic New York jogging route is the nearly 10km circuit of Central Park. If you want a shorter, very scenic alternative, run round the *Jacqueline Kennedy Onassis Reservoir* in the middle of the park. There are also good routes in *Prospect Park* and along the west side of Manhattan.

KAYAKING
Manhattan is surrounded by the Hudson River on the west side and the East River on the east side – and you can kayak on both for free (May-Oct)! Amazing

INSIDER TIP
Paddle around the Big Apple

views of Manhattan from the water are included. *downtownboathouse.org; lic boathouse.org; bbpboathouse.org*

LEISURE CENTRE
The huge 👕 *Chelsea Piers Sports Center (check online for opening times | day ticket $60 | chelseapiers.com | C, E, 1, N, M, F, R or 6th to 23rd Street | 🚇 B9)* at the end of 23rd street offers everything from climbing to bowling, tennis and baseball or pilates.

MORNING WORKOUTS
If you're an early riser and keen to kick-start your morning routine, you can join like-minded folk in this city that never sleeps for a dawn workout. The classes take place outdoors and are free to attend *(therisenyc.org | november-project.com/new-york-ny)*. The city authorities also offer classes: *nycgovparks.org/programs/recreation/ shape-up-nyc.*

Fit for spring: joggers in Central Park

SWIMMING

It's summer, and you need to cool down. Good news! There are lots of open-air public pools in New York, all of which have free entry *(for details, see short.travel/new7)*. Bring a small padlock for your locker, otherwise the very strict staff probably won't let you in.

OFF TO THE STADIUM!

Baseball, basketball, American football – you should visit a big sports stadium in New York at least once. The city's baseball teams are the *Yankees (mlb.com/yankees)*, who play at the Yankee Stadium in the Bronx, and the *Mets (newyorkmets.com)*, who play at Citi Field Stadium in Queens *(April–Sept)*. Basketball fans should head to Madison Square Garden to watch the *Knicks (Nov–May | nba.com/knicks)* or to the Barclays Center to watch the *Brooklyn Nets (nba.com/nets)*. Metlife

Stadium in Meadowlands in New Jersey hosts American football games *(Sept–Dec)* between the *Jets (newyorkjets.com)* and the *Giants (giants.com)*. The *Rangers (nhl.com/rangers)* ice-hockey team and both the *Red Bulls (newyorkredbulls.com)* and *New York City (nycfc.com)* football soccer clubs also attract loyal fans to their games.

YOGA

Lots of New Yorkers seek balance in their hectic lives by practising yoga. Join them at the free sessions that take place between May and October in several New York parks *(e.g. brooklynbridgepark.org/activities/ fitness | bryantpark.org/programs/yoga | socratessculpturepark.org/programs/ all)*. Looking at the Empire State Building while you're doing a "downward-facing dog" is a pretty unique way to experience the city!

FESTIVALS & EVENTS

JANUARY/FEBRUARY

Chinese New Year *(short.travel/new21)*: fireworks and parades all over the city with a focus in Chinatown.

New York Fashion Week *(nyfw.com)*: the famous fashion event lures fashionistas into the city.

MARCH/APRIL

St Patrick's Day *(nycstpatricksparade.org)*: Ireland's patron saint is celebrated on 17 March with a parade on Fifth Avenue, and Guinness galore in the pubs.

Easter Parade *(short.travel/new19)*: barmy bonnets and crazy costumes fill Fifth Avenue on Easter Sunday.

MAY

GreatSaunter*(shorewalkers.org/great-saunter)*: a walk around Manhattan.

Five Boro Bike Tour *(short.travel/new20)*: hire a bike and tour the five boroughs on two wheels.

JUNE

TriBeCa Festival *(tribecafilm.com)*: Hollywood star Robert de Niro is one of the founders of this influential festival in Manhattan's south-western corner.

Museum Mile Festival *(short.travel/new22)*: lots of the museums offer free admission and there's a street party on Fifth Avenue.

Pride Parade *(nycpride.org)*: members of the LGBTQ community in fantastical costumes join New York City's annual Pride march.

JULY

Independence Day: celebrated with fireworks over either the Hudson or East Rivers on the evening of 4th July.

AUGUST

Summer Streets *(nyc.gov/summerstreets)*: ten kilometres of the city's largest avenues are closed to traffic over three Saturdays in August.

A patriotic frenzy of colour: Independence Day fireworks on 4 July

SEPTEMBER

11 September: events to remember the victims of the 9/11 World Trade Center terror attacks in 2001

Steuben Day Parade *(germanparade nyc.org):* German-Americans take over Fifth Avenue to honour the Prussian General Friedrich Wilhelm von Steuben.

San Gennaro *(sangennaro.nyc):* Little Italy becomes food-and-party central to celebrate of the patron saint of Naples.

New York Fashion Week *(nyfw.com):* the Autumn edition of the fashion event.

UN General Assembly *(un.org/en/ga):* world leaders descend on New York for a week of globally important discussions.

New York Film Festival *(filmlinc.org)*

OCTOBER

Halloween *(halloween-nyc.com):* Trick or treat – and a spooky parade in Greenwich Village.

NOVEMBER

New York Marathon *(nyrr.org/tcsnyc marathon)*

Thanksgiving Day Parade *(macys. com/social/parade):* the parade snakes its way down from Central Park and 77th Street to Macy's department store.

Rockefeller Tree Lighting *(rockefeller center.com):* Christmas begins when the lights on the city's largest tree are switched on.

DECEMBER

Park Avenue Christmas Tree Lighting *(short.travel/new23):* fewer lights than Rockefeller but plenty of atmosphere.

New Year's Eve on Times Square *(short.travel/new24):* pop stars, the ball drop, confetti. The party on Times Square is a huge spectacle.

SLEEP WELL

AT HOME WITH THE STARS

The *Greenwich Hotel (75 rooms, 13 suites | 377 Greenwich Street | tel. 1 212 9 41 86 00 | thegreenwichhotel. com | Subway 1 Franklin Street | $$$ | ▥ B15)* in TriBeCa is modern, elegant and tasteful. So it's perhaps no surprise to find out that the famously detail-focused Robert de Niro is its owner.

HOTEL BED AHOY!

The *Jane (211 rooms | 113 Jane Street | tel. 1 212 9 24 67 00 | thejane nyc.com | Subway A, C, E, L 14th Street | $ | ▥ B4)* was originally a hotel for sailors. In 1912 this is where the survivors of the *Titanic* were first accommodated. To this day, some of the rooms look like comfortable cabins.

INSIDER TIP
Sleep in a cabin

ISLAND GLAMPING

In summer you can camp in style at *Collective Governors Island (collective retreats.com/retreat/collective-governors-island | $$ | ▥ D–E21–22)*. There are comfortable beds, a decent restaurant and a campfire every evening with a great view of the Statue of Liberty.

INDUSTRIAL CHIC

The *Paper Factory (123 rooms | 36th Street 3706 | tel. 1 718 3 92 72 00 | short.travel/new25 | Subway M, R 36th Street | $$ | ▥ 0)* in Queens is one of the coolest hotels in the city. It is located in a former factory, decorated with vintage mopeds, a huge tower of books, wooden furniture and leather sofas. There is lots of space and a roof terrace. The subway is just around the corner and only two stops from Manhattan.

INSIDER TIP
Sleeping on the job

In the New York groove: the Standard Hotel

HIGH ABOVE THE HIGH LINE

Rising directly above the High Line, the cool *Standard Hotel (337 rooms | 848 Washington Street | tel. 1 212 6 45 46 46 | short.travel/new16 | Subway A, C, E 14th Street | $$$ | ⌑ B11)* has amazing views of the Hudson River, funky interiors and a great location in the Meatpacking District. Have a cocktail on the roof terrace at *Le Bain*.

SNOOZE IN STYLE

The elegant *Sankofa Aban Bed & Breakfast (6 rooms | 107 Macon Street | tel. 1 917 7 04 92 37 | sankofaaban. com | Subway A, C Nostrand Av. | $$ | ⌑ P23)* is housed in a brownstone built in 1880 in Bedford-Stuyvesant, Brooklyn. The owners have renovated it beautifully.

STAY AT THE YMCA

The Village People were not wrong – New York's YMCAs are still fun places to stay! The rooms are plain but cheap, and there is often a gym and a pool on site too. There are lots of branches in the city, including the central *West Side YMCA (370 beds | 5 W 63rd Street | tel. 1 212 9 12 26 00 | ymcanyc.org/ locations/west-side-ymca/guest rooms | Subway 1, A, B, C, D 59th Street-Columbus Circle | $ | ⌑ F5)*

DISCOVERY TOURS

Do you want to get under the skin of the city? Then these discovery tours provide the perfect guide. They include advice on which sights to visit, tips on where to stop for that perfect holiday snap, a choice of the best places to eat and drink and suggestions for fun activities.

Colourful hustle and bustle: Times Square

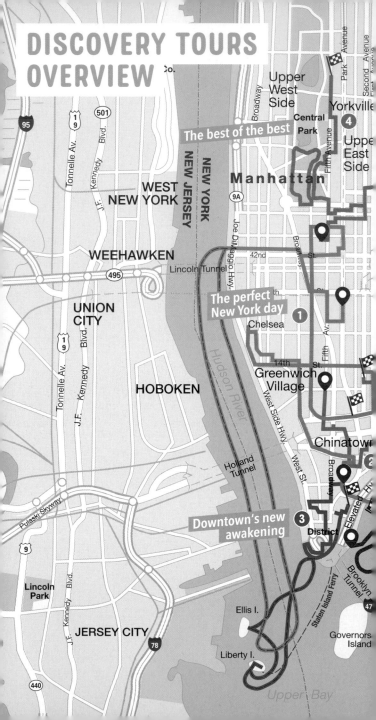

DISCOVERY TOURS OVERVIEW

The best of the best

The perfect New York day **1**

Downtown's new awakening **3**

4

❶ THE PERFECT NEW YORK DAY

➤ Get in the groove and see the most important sights!
➤ Enjoy amazing views of the city
➤ Keep your energy up with some New York specialities

📍 Felix Roasting Co.

🏁 Rockwood Music Hall

→ 30km

🚶 1 day, 3½ hrs total travel/walking time

ℹ️ Get a weekly Metrocard for the subway ($34). "The Beast" speedboat only runs from May to September.

ENERGY BOOST BIG APPLE-STYLE

Due to the time difference, you will probably be starving when you wake up on your first morning in New York. ❶ Felix Roasting Co. *(daily 8am–7pm | 450 Park Av. South | felixroastingco.com | Subway 6 33rd Street)* is one of the nicest cafés in town; it has tasty morsels and very good coffee that is guaranteed to kick-start your day. Once you've refuelled, *walk south on Fifth Avenue to the Flatiron Building (on the right near 23rd Street)* an iconic building in this part of the city, which looks like an upright clothes iron. Shortly thereafter, you will come to ❷ Madison Square Park *(madisonsquarepark. org) on the right-hand side between 23rd and 26th Street* with its modern sculptures.

❶ Felix Roasting Co.

❷ Madison Square Park

AMAZING VIEWS REVEALED

Afterwards, head north to the ❸ Empire State Building ➤ p. 43 on 34th Street. *The lift will whizz up to the viewing platform on the 86th floor*, where the panorama of the city from above will leave you speechless.

❸ Empire State Building

FULL SPEED TO THE STATUE OF LIBERTY

Head in the direction of 42nd Street to reach ❹ Times Square ➤ p. 48. Take in the dazzling lights of the billboards competing for your attention and have a short

❹ Times Square

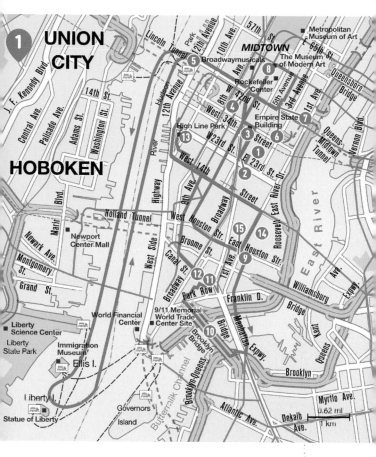

break on the steps in the pedestrianised square. Not for too long mind, as "The Beast", a speedboat run by ⑤ Circle Line Sightseeing Cruises ➤ p. 162 is waiting for you *at its dock on the Hudson River (pier 83, West 42nd Street), about a 20-minute walk away. For half an hour, the boat speeds south, swinging past the Statue of Liberty ➤ p. 35 before turning back.*

A GOAT IN A MUSEUM?

With your adrenalin boosted, walk back to Times Square and take the S-train from there to ⑥ Grand Central Terminal ➤ p. 46. *From the upper level* watch the

⑤ Circle Line
Sightseeing Cruises

⑥ Grand Central
Terminal

crowds of commuters running to the trains. Hungry? At the **❼ Grand Central Dining Concourse** *on the lower level*, there are dozens of dining options serving all kinds of food from around the world. *Back outside, walk along Park Avenue – surrounded by expensive residential buildings – until you come to 53rd Street. Turn left to head to the* **❽ Museum of Modern Art ➤ p. 49.** The lovely Sculpture Garden is home to Picasso's bronze *She-Goat* sculpture.

❼ Grand Central Dining Concourse

❽ Museum of Modern Art

INSIDER TIP
Where Picasso left his goat

TIME FOR A MASSIVE SANDWICH!

Your hunger will have (probably) returned by now, so it's time to indulge in another New York classic experience. *Take the subway to the Lower East Side (M-Train on 53rd Street to 2nd Avenue). Just a few steps away, on Houston Street,* is the famous ★ **❾ Katz's Delicatessen ➤ p. 79**, with its trademark huge pastrami sandwiches.

❾ Katz's Delicatesen

An unforgettable walk over Brooklyn Bridge towards Manhattan

STROLL TO THE SKYLINE

Hop back on the subway and ride to Brooklyn (stop: York Street), so that you can *walk across the* ⑩ Brooklyn Bridge ➤ p. 30. The views are much better starting from this side! The Frank Gehry Tower (8 Spruce Street), glistens at the end of the bridge while the *Statue of Liberty* seems to wave, as ships and ferries of all sizes chug under the bridge.

A SHORT TRIP TO CHINA

Walking though ⑪ Chinatown ➤p. 36 will give you a window into one of New York's communities. Take in the smells, sounds and bustle and glance into the restaurants, food stores and bric-a-brac shops with signs exclusively in Chinese. You'll find handbags, glasses and jewellery on

Frank Gehry's tower, 8 Spruce Street

⑫ Canal Street ➤ p. 36. Time to practise your bartering skills! Also look out for businesses offering a Chinese *massage* to get the knots out of your back and your tired feet. You deserve it!

⑩ Brooklyn Bridge
⑪ Chinatown
⑫ Canal Street

CHILL OUT ABOVE THE STREETS

From Canal Street, take the subway to 14th Street. The charming ⑬ High Line Park ➤ p. 41 was built on the site of a former raised railway. Indigenous grasses grow between the old tracks and wooden deckchairs line the route. There are great views over pretty Greenwich Village with its brownstones – and of the Hudson River and New Jersey on the other side.

⑬ High Line Park

A TASTE OF MOROCCO

Hail a cab and zoom over to the East Village to ⑭ Café Mogador *(Mon–Thu 10am–11pm, Fri 10am–midnight, Sat 9.30am–midnight, Sun 9.30am–11pm | 101 St Marks Place | cafemogador.com).* Delicious Moroccan creations and a hip crowd are the perfect combination to start your New York evening in style.

⑭ Café Mogador

AMERICAN ROCK

⑮ Rockwood Music Hall

Any energy left? Then *walk a couple of blocks south to the* ⑮ Rockwood Music Hall ➤ p. 115, a club popular with undiscovered musicians. Order a drink and enjoy the intimate atmosphere and some good music.

❷ IMMIGRANT CITY

➤ Understand Manhattan's immigrant heritage
➤ Wander through little China, Italy and Ukraine
➤ Delicious food and amazing architecture everywhere you look

📍 Washington Square

🏁 Veselka

➡ 4km

🚶 6 hrs, 1 hr total walking time

TRIUMPHAL ARCH, CHATTING STUDENTS

❶ Washington Square

Start at ❶ Washington Square ➤ p. 39, with its victory arch where students from the neighbouring New York University (NYU) often hang out and buskers strut their stuff. Fancy testing your brain? Chess players congregate in the southwest corner. Feel free to join a game and try to bamboozle your opponent. *Cross over Bleecker Street*, the centre of the folk music scene since the 1960s, *and follow West Houston Street to one of the city's most interesting architectural districts:* ❷ SoHo ➤ p. 36. Some of the cast-iron buildings – once large factories, shops and warehouses – still line the old cobblestone streets. They were converted into lofts by artists and students in the 1960s; you can explore one that was once lived in by sculptor Donald Judd (*juddfoundation.org*). *Wander along Spring Street*, browse in the boutiques and do a little people-watching while you are there.

❷ SoHo

IT'S GONNA GET GLAM

❸ Broadway

Spring Street runs into ❸ Broadway ➤ p. 37 at its

eastern end where there are plenty of shops. *Walk uptown and pop into* Prada ➤ p. 99, *before turning round and walking back southwards. Return to the popular celeb hangout Spring Street.* Those looking to upscale their Instagram feed or to catch a glimpse of an A-list celebrity, should pop into the bistro ❹ Balthazar ➤ p. 107.

❹ Balthazar

FROM ITALY TO CHINA

Walk two blocks to the east on Spring Street and then go right onto Mulberry Street, the main street of ❺ Little Italy ➤ p. 36. Overlooking the cluster of Italian

❺ Little Italy

restaurants are late 19th-century tenement buildings with their distinctive fire escapes. Little Italy is getting smaller because **⑥ Chinatown** ➤ p. 36 is expanding to the north. Canal Street is the centre of the Chinese market for fish, meat and vegetables, with stall holders letting you try before you buy.

⑥ Chinatown

DUMPLING TIME TRAVEL

Turn left down Bowery Street, then follow Grand Street and Orchard Street to another district in the midst of gentrification: the **⑦ Lower East Side** ➤ p. 39. Jewish immigrants from Eastern Europe dominated this part of the city in the 19th century. Synagogues, grocery shops and restaurants still attest to their influence, but hip bars, restaurants and boutiques have pushed out much of the Jewish community. *Make sure to visit the* **⑧ Yonah Schimmel Knish Bakery** *(daily 10am–7pm | 137 E Houston Street | knishery.com)* and try a spinach *knish*, a savoury Eastern European filled dumpling – a taste of the old Lower East Side.

⑦ Lower East Side

⑧ Yonah Schimmel Knish Bakery

LITTLE GERMANY IN THE EAST VILLAGE

To the north of Houston Street, the contrasts continue. Beginning in the 1850s, many German immigrants moved into simple apartments in the heart of the **⑨ East Village** ➤ p. 39, earning it the nickname "Little Germany". *Avenue A* and *Tompkins Square Park* were a stronghold of the hippies in the 1960s and of the punk rock scene in the 1970s. Today this neighbourhood is still home to students and creatives but also celebs, bankers and lawyers.

⑨ East Village

INSIDER TIP
The best ki▮
of shoppin▮

One of the last stops for the day is **⑩ St Marks Place** ➤ p. 42, with its attractive little boutiques. *When you reach Second Avenue, head north. At* **⑪ Veselka** ➤ p. 80 *on the corner of Ninth Street,* the food is Russian-Ukrainian. Never tried it? Then order some delicious *blintzes* – pancakes with a cream cheese filling.

⑩ St Marks Place

⑪ Veselka

Some places in Little Italy still look like part of a film set

③ DOWNTOWN'S NEW AWAKENING

➤ Take time to remember the victims of 9/11
➤ Look down over Manhattan
➤ Climb up to the Statue of Liberty's crown

📍	Municipal Building	🏁	South Street Seaport
→	4km	🚶	6 hrs, 1 hr total travel/walking time

ⓘ It is best to book your tickets for Liberty Island online so as to reduce your queuing time.

CONTEMPLATE THE HORRORS OF 9/11

From the ❶ Municipal Building *(1 Centre Street), located on subway line R, walk to Duane Park.* The antique shops you find here today will give you an impression of how the merchants who built up the

❶ Municipal Building

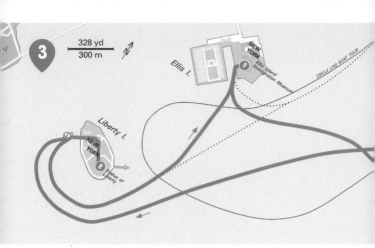

southern tip of Manhattan in the late 18th century once lived. *The corner of Duane Street and Broadway is home to the* ❷ African Burial Ground *(290 Broadway | nps.gov/afbg),* an old cemetery in which an estimated 15,000 slaves from Africa are buried. You can learn more about the history of this site, first rediscovered in 1991, at the

❷ African Burial Ground

> **INSIDER TIP**
> A grim chap
> ter in NYC'
> history

Visitors' Center. *From here, walk further south to New York's City Hall* ➤ p. 30, built between 1803 and 1812. *The nearby Woolworth Building (233 Broadway/ between Barclay Street and Park Place),* with its green copper tip is a real eye-catcher.

❸ St Paul's Chapel

Manhattan's only colonial era church, ❸ St Paul's Chapel ➤ p. 33, *is located on Vesey Street.* This small chapel was a saving grace for exhausted helpers during the World Trade Center attacks. *Walk along Vesey Street to get to Ground Zero,* now the site of the ❹ 9/11 Memorial ➤ p. 32, with its two dark pools bearing the engraved names of all the victims. Take a moment to reflect and listen to the water falling in this special space. You get a good view of One World Trade Center ➤ p. 32 from here too. The ❺ One World Observatory *(oneworldobservatory.com)* is the highest observation deck in the city.

❹ 9/11 Memorial

❺ One World Observatory

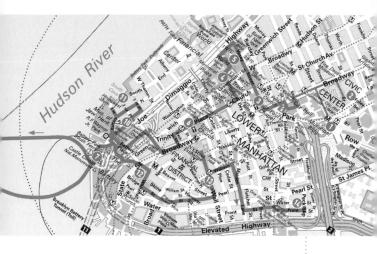

LADY LIBERTY HOLDS COURT

Back at ground level, *walk south on Church Street, past*
❻ Trinity Church, which crouches between the tall
buildings of the financial district. Shortly before you
come to the southern end of Broadway, the famous
charging bronze bull on Wall Street, symbolising a
strong, optimistic financial market, scrapes at the
ground with his hooves. The view down the tree-lined
avenue running south from *Battery Place* and *First Place*
is fantastic. You can capture one of New York's most
famous landmarks – the *Statue of Liberty* – together
with Ellis Island and Verrazano Bridge in one shot. *You
can get even closer to Lady Liberty by heading to*
❼ Castle Clinton, where immigrants to the New World
were received until 1860, to *board the ferry to the*
❽ Statue of Liberty ➤ p. 34. Enjoy the view before
climbing up to the viewing platform in the crown – but
remember, you'll need to book tickets for this well in
advance. *Continue on to* **❾ Ellis Island** ➤ p. 34, the
island which served as a reception centre for immigrants after 1860.

| ❻ Trinity Church |
| ❼ Castle Clinton |
| ❽ Statue of Liberty |
| ❾ Ellis Island |

MONEY, MONEY, MONEY

*Back on the mainland, you can decide whether you
want to visit one of the three museums that you will
pass on your way through Battery Park to Wall Street:*

⑩ The Skyscraper Museum, the ⑪ Museum of Jewish Heritage (➤ both p. 33) or the ⑫ National Museum of the American Indian ➤ p. 34. Then delve into the financial world. *At the corner of Broad Street and Pearl Street, look for* Fraunces Tavern *(54 Pearl Street | tel. 1 212 9 68 17 76 | frauncestavern.com | $$–$$$)*, a restaurant established in 1763 famous for its New York strip steak. *From Pearl Street, turn left down* ⑬ Wall Street ➤ p. 33, home of the New York Stock Exchange.

A STYLISH WAY TO END A DAY

Take Pine Street to Chase Manhattan Plaza, the first skyscraper built in the international style of the 1960s, *then cross over Water Street on Maiden Lane,* which was flanked with bars and brothels in the 19th century. At the end of it, *you will come to the pleasant historic* ⑭ South Street Seaport district, where you can end the day in style, perhaps at the Japanese restaurant Suteishi *(24 Peck Slip | tel. 1 212 7 66 23 44 | suteishi. com | $–$$)*.

Remembering a national trauma: on the way to the 9/11 Memorial

❹ THE BEST OF THE BEST

➤ Enjoy time in Central Park
➤ Explore some of the world's best museums
➤ Hit the posh shops or at least admire their displays

📍 Rockefeller Center

🏁 Guggenheim Museum

→ 4.5km

🚶 7 hrs, 2 hrs total travel/walking time

ℹ️ The Roosevelt Island Tram is included on your Metrocard.

SHOP TIL YOU DROP …

Prometheus can be found in the centre of Manhattan, surrounded by a huge office and shopping complex walked through by 250,000 people each day. Named after John D. Rockefeller, who commissioned them, the 14 buildings of ❶ Rockefeller Center ➤ p. 47 were built in 1929 *between 48th and 51st Street on Fifth Avenue*. The golden Prometheus sculpture, which represents democracy, progress and global understanding, is part of the decorative square beneath *30 Rockefeller Plaza. From here, take a little detour to the north to the venerable department store* ❷ Saks Fifth Avenue ➤ p. 93, with its huge cosmetics department. Treat yourself to a little makeover from a make-up pro.

… AND THEN FLOAT AWAY

Freshly made up, you're ready to face world of fashion – from Versace to Gap – in shops *that line the sidewalks of Fifth Avenue. Go back to 55th Street and turn left to head north along Madison Avenue. Check out the lobby of* ❸ 550 Madison Avenue ➤ p. 49, the former Sony Building, then *head east to the station for the* ❹ Roosevelt Island Tramway ➤ p. 50: *Drift over the East River in a cable car before you return to the*

INSIDER TIP
Fly over the city

❶ Rockefeller Center

❷ Saks Fifth Avenue

❸ 550 Madison Avenue

❹ Roosevelt Island Tramway

glamorous world of Fifth Avenue – and the sparkling jewellery in the windows at ➎ Tiffany & Co. ➤ p. 101.

➎ Tiffany & Co.

STRAWBERRY FIELDS FOREVER

You should definitely at least *wander through the lower floors of the upmarket department store* ➏ Bergdorf Goodman ➤ p. 92. Unwind from your shopping spree with a stop in the green expanses of ➐ Central Park ➤ p. 51. Rent a bike from the inexpensive ➑ Citi Bike ➤ p. 156 scheme and pootle through the park. Hot dog stands are set up all over – so treat yourself. ➒ Strawberry Fields, a garden honouring the

➏ Bergdorf Goodman

➐ Central Park
➑ Citi Bike

memory of John Lennon, is *located in the park at 72nd Street West in front of the* Dakota ➤ p. 55

⑨ Strawberry Fields

EXCLUSIVE & ARTISTIC

After this little detour, head straight through the park to upper Fifth Avenue, home to some of the most luxurious apartments in the city and some of the most interesting museums in the world. The **⑩ Frick Collection** ➤ p. 51 *on the corner of 70th Street* is housed in an elegant fin-de-siecle townhouse. Closed for renovations at the time of writing, it's due to reopen in 2024. *Head back to* **⑪** Madison Avenue ➤ p. 46. This is the street's most exclusive section, lined with expensive fashion boutiques. *When you get to 80th Street, walk back to Fifth Avenue, past the* Metropolitan Museum of Art ➤ p. 52, with its huge open staircase, *towards 86th Street and the* ⑫ Neue Galerie New York

⑩ Frick Collection

⑪ Madison Avenue

⑫ Neue Galerie New York

Imagine: remembering John Lennon

➤ p. 53, which displays early 20th-century German and Austrian art. Top off the exquisite art with a bit of Viennese coffeehouse flair in the museum café, which serves delicious apple strudel. It seems fitting to end the tour with an architectural highlight; *just three blocks away is the* ⑬ Guggenheim Museum ➤ p. 54, Frank Lloyd Wright's great masterpiece.

⑬ Guggenheim Museum

⑤ BEAUTIFUL BROOKLYN

➤ Relax by the river in Brooklyn Bridge Park
➤ Marvel at the classic and modern architecture
➤ Take a break at the fairground

📍 NYC Ferry	🏁	Bargemusic
→ 3.5km	🚶	8 hrs, 3 hrs total walking time

ℹ Bring swimming stuff.
Good to know: the kayaks at Brooklyn Bridge Park are handed out on a first-come, first-served basis and there are a limited number! Bargemusic is only open on Fri and Sat. ❸ AlMar is closed on Sun.

FROM THE CAROUSEL TO THE KAYAKS

① NYC Ferry
② Dumbo
③ AlMar

④ Powerhouse Arena

⑤ Main Street Park

The ① NYC Ferry *(S Street | Pier 11 | ferry.nyc) will bring you to* ② Dumbo ➤ p. 60, *where the café* ③ AlMar ➤ p. 72 will serve you a delicious breakfast. The former factory buildings and warehouses in this part of Brooklyn have been converted into apartments, offices, designer shops and restaurants. *Go into* ④ Powerhouse Arena ➤ p. 90 *on the corner of Water and Main Street,* a huge bookstore with regular exhibitions and events. *Continue towards the water on Main Street until you come to* ⑤ Main Street Park. At the little beach, enjoy the very best view of the Brooklyn Bridge with the Manhattan skyline in

INSIDER TIP
The best view of the Manhattan skyline

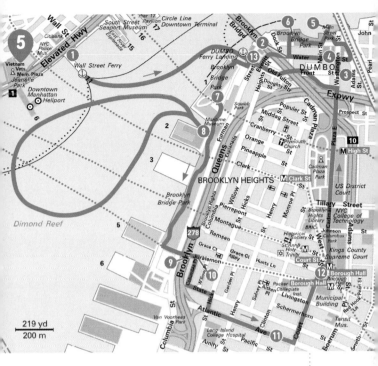

the background! On the left-hand side, you will see a historic gem housed in a glass pavilion: ⑥ Jane's Carousel (*janescarousel.com*), which was built in 1922. It costs just \$2 to ride its pretty horses. The next bit of the walk is absolutely lovely. ⑦ Brooklyn Bridge Park (*brooklynbridgepark.org*) *stretches along the East River to the south*. It has a lot to offer: paths lead over little hills and through mini copses, while the pretty piers play host to sports such as basketball, petanque, beach volleyball, soccer and roller skating. Time for lunch? There are good restaurants at the top of Old Fulton Street. Rent a kayak for free at the ⑧ Brooklyn Bridge Park Boathouse (*June–Aug Wed/Thu 5–7pm, Sat 10am–3pm, Sun noon–2.30pm | Pier 2 | bbpboathouse. org*) and *explore New York from the water* – an unforgettable experience! *Back on land*, stretch out on the grass or take a dip in the pool with a view of Manhattan and the *Statue of Liberty*, as the seagulls screech overhead.

⑥ Jane's Carousel

⑦ Brooklyn Bridge Park

⑧ Brooklyn Bridge Park Boathouse

LIVING IN A WRITER'S PARADISE

Walk down to Joralemon Street on the left and then head uphill to the historic district of ⑨ Brooklyn Heights ➤ p. 60. *On the corner of Columbia Place, you will find the* ⑩ River Deli *(daily from 5pm | 32 Joralemon Street | riverdelirestaurant.com | $$$), a charming Italian restaurant. After a gastronomic break, continue uphill and turn left on Hicks Street and left again on Remsen Street*, passing tree-lined rows of elegant brownstones. This picturesque part of Brooklyn has been home to many 20th-century American writers, such as Truman Capote, Henry and Arthur Miller, Paul Bowles and Carson McCullers.

⑨ **Brooklyn Heights**

⑩ **River Deli**

A TASTE OF THE MIDDLE EAST

Head on to Atlantic Avenue. This shopping street has many designer boutiques, antique shops, restaurants and the popular Arabic deli ⑪ Sahadi's *(closed Sun | Atlantic Av. 187 | sahadis. com)* which has the charm of an old grocery store. Try some of the olives or one of the 150 different kinds of cheese!

⑪ **Sahadi's**

INSIDER TIP
Delicious deli delights

The best Arabic smells and tastes at Sahadi's

A slam dunk plus a skyline in Brooklyn Bridge Park

Just half a block to the east, turn left on Court Street until you come to ⑫ Brooklyn Borough Hall, the borough's impressive former government building, built in 1848. Walk along Cadman Plaza Park for about 20 minutes to get back to Brooklyn Bridge where a treat awaits, in the form of a concert at ⑬ Bargemusic ➤ p. 120 awaits – classical music in front of the gleaming backdrop of Manhattan.

⑫ Brooklyn Borough Hall

⑬ Bargemusic

GOOD TO KNOW

CITY BREAK BASICS

GETTING THERE

ARRIVAL

Flights to New York from the UK take 7-8 hours and most land at *John F. Kennedy Airport (JFK)* in Queens. From there you can take a taxi into the city *($52 flat rate, or $56.50 during rush hour, plus toll und 15–20% tip | journey time approx. 1 hr)*. Warning: only take the official taxis, i.e. the yellow cabs. Other taxi drivers may offer you a cheaper ride, but these are best avoided.

Shuttle buses are a good-value alternative – but are only available with an online reservation in advance: try *New York Airport Shuttle (goairlinkshuttle.com)* or *Super Shuttle (supershuttle.com)*.

The cheapest option is the subway. Take the *Airtrain (travel time 12 mins | $7.75 | jfkairport.com)* from the terminal to Howard Beach Station. Change trains and take the A train to Manhattan *(travel time approx. 1½ hrs | Metrocard $2.75)*. Note: on the return journey take an "A" train towards Far Rockaway/

– 5 hours behind GMT

The USA changes its clocks in summer and winter on different dates to the UK, so the time difference drops to just four hours for much of autumn and spring.

Adapter Type A

110 volt/60 Hz adapter

New York taxis will take you through the city's busy streets

Mott Avenue and Rockaway Park Beach and get off at the Howard Beach–JFK Airport Station. Or, on arrival, take the Airtrain to Jamaica Station *($7.75)* and change trains to the faster Long Island Rail Road *(travel time 20 mins | from $7.75)* to Penn Station; this is ideal if you arrive at JFK during *rush hour*.

If your flight arrives at *Newark (EWR)* in New Jersey, take the *Newark Airport Express Bus* to Midtown Manhattan *(every 20-30 mins | travel time 1 hr | $17, return trip $30 | coachusa.com)*. Or take the Airtrain to Newark Airport Station, then head on to Penn Station *(travel time 45 mins– 1 hr | $15 | newarkairport.com)* on a normal train. A taxi will take you about 1 hr and cost approx. $50 plus tip. A surcharge of $17.50 is applicable on taxi rides *out* of New York.

National flights often arrive at the city's third hub, *La Guardia (LGA)* in Queens. To reach Manhattan, there are a number of options: the NYC Airport Express bus *(travel time approx. 45 mins | c. $40)*; the Super Shuttle *(travel time approx. 1 hr | $40)*; the free public bus service Q70, which runs to 74th Street/Roosevelt Avenue Subway station, from where you can pick up Subway lines 7, E, F, M and R for your onward journey, or a taxi *(journey time approx. 45 mins | $50 plus tip)*.

IMMIGRATION

To travel to the United States you need a machine-readable passport with a digital chip containing biometric information, valid for the duration of your stay.

You must register for an ESTA Visa Waiver *(https://esta.cbp.dhs.gov)* before departure. The application costs $14 and is valid for two years in which time you can enter the USA as often as you like (for less than 90 days).

GETTING AROUND

PUBLIC TRANSPORT

The best way to get around New York is on foot or via the subway and buses.

The price for a single trip is $2.75 no matter the distance. You enter stations using a magnetic card, the *Metrocard*, which has a number of advantages: free transfers between the subway and buses, bulk discounts and a weekly ticket for $33, which is especially good for tourists who are staying long enough. The *Metrocard* is obtainable from machines in subway stations. You can pay with cash on buses but, be prepared, as you'll need exactly $2.75 in change! It is also possible to access the One Metro New York (OMNY) System by using your credit card or mobile phone and tapping it on the sensor as you enter and exit the network. One special feature of New York's subway system are the express trains which don't stop at every station (unlike the local trains). Some stations have different entrances on opposite sides of the street for trains travellling Uptown or Downtown. The subway network is constantly under construction and there are often lines closed or detours in operation (mainly at the weekend). For information, listen to announcements or go to *mta.info*.

If the weather is nice, the ferries are a great way to travel. The network is growing and getting more comfortable *(ferry.nyc)*.

TAXIS

You can always hail a yellow cab on the street. Taxis in New York are relatively affordable and can be booked using the *Curb* app. The basic fee is $2.50 and each fifth of a mile after that costs $0.50. A journey of about 25 blocks costs $10 (not including a tip of around 20%). There is a $0.50 surcharge at night from 8pm–6am and a $1 surcharge during rush hour (5–8pm). Any tolls also have to be paid by the customer.

In competition with the public transport services, there are now also a huge range of ride-hailing apps, including *Uber*, *Lyft* and *Via*.

BIKE HIRE

You will now find blue *Citi Bike (citibikenyc.com)* stations across the city. A single ride of up to 30 mins costs $3.99 and for $15 you can have unlimited rides up to 30 mins for 24 hours. The network now includes e-bikes. Be careful: New York is still not really a cycling city and bikes often have to play second fiddle to cars and pedestrians.

CAR HIRE

If you are planning to travel on from New York by car, it is best to get your hire car at the airport where you will get cheaper deals (from $50/day); obviously, it is even cheaper to book in advance before you travel. One thing to remember, however, is that parking is a huge problem in Manhattan. There are too few spaces, and the risk of break-ins and theft means that your best option is to use an expensive

Get around the city on two wheels with Citi Bike

private car park (daily rates approx $50). Chauffeur-driven limos or town cars (from $80 per hr for a minimum of 1½ hrs, plus 20% tip and tax) are provided by *Avalon (tel. 1 800 5 28 25 66 | avalontrans.com)*.

EMERGENCIES

CONSULATES & EMBASSIES
BRITISH CONSULATE GENERAL
845 3rd Av. | tel. 1 212 7 45 02 00 | www.ukinusa.fco.gov.uk | Subway 6 51st Street
CANADIAN CONSULATE
Mon–Fri 9–5pm | 1251 Avenue of the Americas | tel. 1 212 596 16 28 | can-am.gc.ca/new-york | Subway F 47–50th Street

IRISH CONSULATE GENERAL
345 Park Avenue, 17th Floor | tel. 1 212 319 25 55 | www.consulate ofirelandnewyork.org | Subway 6 51st Street-Lexington Av.

EMERGENCY
The emergency number for police and medical assistance is 911 (free from public phones).

HEALTH
Make sure your travel insurance covers the USA for healthcare. Accident and emergency departments (called *emergency rooms* or *ER*) are obliged to treat all patients, but they demand a credit card from non-US citizens. If you need basic help, CityMD practices are all over the city, and you can turn up without an appointment *(citymd.com)*.

ESSENTIALS

New York is expensive. Finding hotel rooms for under $100 per night is rare – the average is $300–400. One reason for this is that the city receives 65 million visitors each year, meaning supply is scarce, so book early (the best deals are normally online). There are seasonal variations too: January, February, July and August are generally the cheapest months.

Prices are always quoted for the room not the person. Doubles generally don't cost much more than a single. Watch out for tax; your quote won't include sales tax, city tax or the $3.50 hotel tax. It can be cheaper to find a package deal including your flights. For more information on hotels, look online and use the popular booking portals.

Given how expensive hotels are, it is not surprising that many visitors book apartments and rooms from private individuals. Alongside *airbnb. com*, *nyhabitat.com* can help you find a good deal where you want to be. If you're hoping to stay a bit longer, check out the newsletter by *listings project.com*.

CUSTOMS

You cannot bring plants, fresh food or jams/pickles etc into the USA. 200

One of the city's best addresses: Fifth Avenue

cigarettes (or 50 cigars/2 kg tobacco), 1l of spirits and gifts up to a value of $100 are allowed. When shopping for souvenirs, check your allowances carefully. You don't want to have to pay large customs fees when you get home.

EVENTS LISTINGS

There are events listings in the *New York Times (nytimes.com)*, the *New York Post (nypost.com)* and in *Daily News (nydailynews.com)*. *New York Magazine (nymag.com)* lists cultural and sporting events while *The New Yorker (newyorker.com)* also has cinema and club listings. *Time Out (timeout.com)* has the best music listings and *Village Voice (villagevoice. com)* includes political events in its round ups. *flavorpill.com* is also very up to date.

INFORMATION

The *Official NYC Information Center (Mon–Sat 10am–10pm, Sun 10am–9pm | 151 W 34th Street | short.travel/ new17 | Subway B, D, F, M, N, Q, R 34th Street-Herald Square | ⊞ E9)* provides comprehensive tourist information and can advise about the many different discounts on offer. For an overview, consult *freetoursbyfoot.com/new-york-city-passes*.

INTERNET ACCESS & WIFI

The city is in the process of installing thousands of internet points with fast WiFi, telephones and USB charging points all over the city. *(link.nyc)*. Most libraries, parks, subway stations and museums have free WiFi as do many cafés and hotels.

HOW MUCH DOES IT COST?

Espresso	*$2.50 for a cup*
Hot dog	*$2 for a hot dog at Nathan's, Coney Island*
Cinema	*from $12 per ticket in Manhattan*
Soft drink	*$1.50 for bottled water/Coca Cola*
Taxi	*$10 approx for a short trip (2 miles)*
Subway	*$2.75 per ticket*

MONEY, BANKS & CREDIT CARDS

1 dollar = 100 cents. *Bills* come in the following denominations: one, five, ten, 20, 50, 100 dollars. *Coins* in denominations of one, five, ten, 25, 50 cents and one dollar. Coins may also be referred to as follows: *penny* (1 cent), *nickel* (5 cents), *dime* (10 cents) and *quarter* (25 cents). The proverbial *buck* equals one dollar.

Credit cards are the most popular method of payment. You can get cash at an ATM in banks, delis and drugstores. Check whether you need to inform your bank that you are going away (or transactions may be blocked) and whether they have a partner institution in the US for free cash withdrawals. For the current exchange rate go to, for example, *oanda.com (short.travel/new31)*.

NATIONAL HOLIDAYS

1 Jan	New Year's Day
Last Mon in May	Memorial Day
4 July	Independence Day
First Mon in Sept	Labor Day
Fourth Thu in Nov	Thanksgiving
25 Dec	Christmas Day

PHONE & MOBILE PHONE

In New York the area code is always included in a phone number and to call from a mobile you need to put a "1" before it (the numbers in this book are all written so you don't need to think about this). From a foreign phone you need to add the dialling code 00. Information *Tel. 4 11 (*)* ($ 0,50 per request) and *411.com*. To call out of America you have to dial 011 and then the country area code without the "+" or "00". For the UK, this means 011-44. Then skip the first "0" of the number.

Your own mobile phone should work in the USA using the roaming network, but this may be very expensive so it is always worth considering buying a SIM card from a US phone company for your sta. There are also small differences in frequencies on US networks; T-Mobile US and AT&T SIM cards work reliably on European phones but always double check before you buy. You can buy pay-as-you-go cards at kiosks and supermarkets. Some European companies (e.g. *usapayasyougosimcard. co.uk*) can arrange US SIM cards before your departure too. Hotels often charge shocking fees for international calls (up $1.50/min) so use apps that work on Wi-i instead, such as *WhatsApp* or *Skype*.

POST

You can find the nearest post office at *usps.com*. Stamps can also be purchased at machines, in souvenir shops and at some delis. A postcard to Europe costs $1.15; there are blue post boxes all over the city.

PUBLIC TOILETS

Public "rest rooms" are a scarce commodity in New York. That said, lobbies accessible to the general public in a number of skyscrapers and shopping centres often have toilets. Another alternative are the toilets located in the lobbies of big hotels, in department stores, in bookstores and in outlets of Starbucks and McDonald's. The best and cleanest public bathrooms are in Bryant Park.

SIGHTSEEING TOURS

There are good sightseeing tours by bus with companies, including *New York Sightseeing (tel. 1 212 4 45 08 48 | newyorksightseeing.com | ⊞ E8)* Alongside lots of options in the city, they also take tourists on outings to, for example, Woodbury Outlet *(from $47).* They have stops all over the city.

Harlem Spirituals (tel. 1 212 3 91 09 00 | harlemspirituals.com) run tours in Harlem. On Sundays, these include a visit to a Baptist Church *($75).*

You'd rather see things from up high? *Liberty Helicopters (6 E River Greenway | tel. 1 212 7 86 57 51 | libertyhelicopters.com | Subway N, R Whitehall Street | ⊞ B18)* will fly you around the Manhattan skyline *(12–15 mins. $229 per person, 17–20 mins $279 per person). HeliNY (tel. 1 212 3 55 08 01 | heliny.com)* at the same location charges almost exactly the same.

Entrance to the Circle Line Sightseeing Cruise at Pier 83 on the Hudson River

In the midst of a sea of lights: taxis in Times Square

Manhattan is surrounded by water, so boat tours are a great option too. Particularly popular are the 3-hr tours run by *Circle Line Sightseeing Cruises (mid-April–Oct daily 10am–3.30pm, in winter once a day | Pier 83/W 42nd Street/Hudson River and Pier 16/South Street Seaport | price $44 | tel. 1 212 5 63 32 00 | circleline.com | Subway A, C, E 42nd Street-Port Authority | ⊞ C7)*. Night tours are especially atmospheric *(Harbour Lights | from $44)*, as you take in the lights of the skyscrapers.

Dinner cruises (unsurprisingly) focus on food and are offered by companies including *Bateaux Dinner Cruise (daily, boarding 7pm | Pier 61, Chelsea Piers | from $164.90 | tel. 1 855 6 47 97 14 | short.travel/new27 | Subway C, E, 1, N, M, F, R or 6 to 23rd Street | ⊞ C7)*. You won't forget the experience of watching the moon rise over the *Statue of Liberty* while you tuck into a delicious meal.

Companies like *Big Apple Greeter (bigapplegreeter.org)* and *Free Tours by Foot (freetoursbyfoot.com)* offer very cheap or even free walking tours.

INSIDER TIP
Tour with the locals

TICKETS

Shows sell out quickly so booking online in advance is generally better than calling the box office while there. Ticket agents add a surcharge to the ticket price but are available 24 hours: *Telecharge (tel. 1 212 2 39 62 00 | tele charge.com)* and *Ticketmaster (tel. 1 800 7 45 30 00 | ticketmaster.com)*.

Often hotel concierges will be able to assist you. Remember to tip them commensurate with services rendered. Reduced price tickets for same day shows can be obtained from: *TKTS (Mon, Tue, Fri 3–8pm, Wed, Thu, Sat 11am–8pm, Sun 11am–7pm | $2 service charge | tdf.org | Broadway/47th Street | ⊞ E7)*

TIPPING

In the USA, tipping is not only welcomed, it is expected – and often constitutes a large proportion of the service-provider's income. In restaurants the rule of thumb dictates that you multiply the tax by two to work out a tip. You can normally add tip on a card very easily. Always check the bill though; some restaurants worry that foreigners don't tip, so they add an automatic "gratuity".

Wine waiters and maître d's should be tipped extra for especially good service (such as holding a particular table for you – at least $10 or $20 in a smarter place). Bell boys should get at least $1 per piece of luggage or up to $5 in very smart hotels. Hotel maids should get about $5 a day (this can be reduced for very long stays) Concierges should get a generous tip for helping you with things like theatre tickets. Taxi drivers will expect about 15%.

WEIGHTS & MEASURES

The USA exclusively uses Imperial weights and measures. While the length (mile, foot, inch) and weight (pound, ounce) measures may be familiar to a British audience, volumes measured in gallons (3.78 litres) and quarts (0.94 litres) will be more novel – and just to confuse you, American pints are about 100ml smaller than British ones. Clothes sizes are also different. A good rule of thumb is that US sizes are two smaller than UK ones, but it is always worth trying items on before you buy them.

WEATHER IN NEW YORK

High season
Low season

	JAN	FEB	MARCH	APRIL	MAY	JUNE	JULY	AUG	SEPT	OCT	NOV	DEC
Daytime temperature	$4°$	$5°$	$9°$	$14°$	$21°$	$25°$	$28°$	$27°$	$24°$	$18°$	$12°$	$6°$
Night-time temperature	$-4°$	$-4°$	$0°$	$5°$	$11°$	$17°$	$19°$	$19°$	$16°$	$10°$	$4°$	$-2°$
☀	4	6	7	8	8	10	9	8	8	6	5	4
🌂	8	7	9	9	8	7	7	7	6	5	8	8
≋	3	2	4	8	13	18	22	23	21	17	11	6

☀ Hours of sunshine per day　🌂 Rainy days per month　≋ Water temperature in °C

The Vessel, a permanent art installation at Hudson Yards

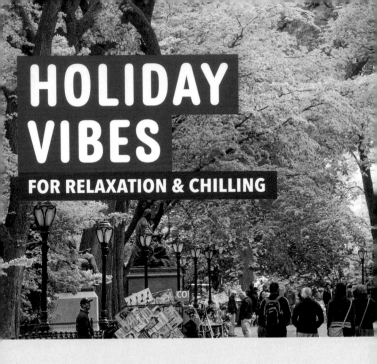

HOLIDAY VIBES
FOR RELAXATION & CHILLING

FOR BOOKWORMS & FILM BUFFS

📖 HERE IS NEW YORK

E.B. White's love letter to NYC is just 50 pages long, but it remains just as touching and relevant 70 years after he wrote it.

📖 OPEN CITY

The Nigerian-American writer and photographer Teju Cole tells the story of Julius, a Nigerian immigrant, who wanders around the city after quitting his psychology degree and splitting up with his girlfriend. One of the most atmospheric and beautiful recent books about New York (2011).

🎥 THE LANDLORD

Cult 1970s comedy about very early gentrification in Brooklyn's Park Slope. Directed by Hal Ashby.

🎥 THE MARVELOUS MRS. MAISEL

Largely shot on the Upper West Side, this TV series on Amazon Prime tells the story of Miriam Maisel, a Jewish housewife and mother who leaves her husband and starts a new career as a stand-up comedian in 1950s New York.

PLAYLIST
BIG-APPLE-GROOVE

0:58

**II JAY-Z & ALICIA KEYS –
EMPIRE STATE OF MIND**
THE New York anthem

**▶ DUKE ELLINGTON –
TAKE THE A TRAIN**
The classic jazz tune

**▶ JONI MITCHELL –
CHELSEA MORNING**
The best depiction of Chelsea's atmosphere in music

**▶ SIMON & GARFUNKEL –
A HEART IN NEW YORK**
Recorded live in Central Park, this is a great way to get in the mood for the Big Apple

**▶ ELLA FITZGERALD – MANHATTAN
& AUTUMN IN NEW YORK**
Two definitive songs to understand the metropolis

**▶ ACE FREHLEY –
NEW YORK GROOVE**
Captures the sound of the city

Your holiday soundtrack can be found on **Spotify** under **MARCO POLO New York**

Or scan this code with the Spotify app

ONLINE

UNTAPPED CITIES
A young couple has made getting to know every nook and cranny of the city their goal in life, and they share their discoveries on their blog (they offer tours too): *untappedcities.com*

HUMANS OF NEW YORK
In 2010 Brandon Stanton decided to photograph 10,000 New Yorkers on the streets; soon after, he started interviewing them too. HONY now enjoys cult status: *humansofnewyork.com*

FOODBABY NY
From cucumber ice cream to cronuts, New Yorkers are always trying inventive new foods. Mike Chau has made a business of this by taking his three kids around the city trying new tastes. He has over 300,000 of foodie followers on Instagram *@foodbabyny*

NEW YORK TODAY
Find out what is happening each day in the Big Apple. This *New York Times* newsletter will keep you right up to date: *nytimes.com/column/ny-today-daily-briefings*

TRAVEL PURSUIT

THE MARCO POLO HOLIDAY QUIZ

Do you know what makes New York tick? Test your knowledge of the idiosyncrasies and eccentricities of the city and its people. You will find the answers at the foot of the page, with more detailed explanations on pages 20 to 25.

❶ What services do New York's doormen provide?
a) Calling taxis, taking in packages, holding doors
b) Making and repairing doors
c) Giving dating tips

❷ Which building is New York's tallest and also the tallest in the western hemisphere?
a) Empire State Building in Midtown
b) Chrysler Building in Midtown
c) One World Trade Center in Lower Manhattan

❸ And how tall is it?
a) 541m
b) 402m
c) 657m

❹ Which of these is the only one of New York's boroughs to be entirely on the United States mainland?
a) Brooklyn
b) Manhattan
c) The Bronx

❺ Broadway, Off-Broadway, Off-Off-Broadway – what's the difference?
a) The location of the theatre: on Broadway or on a side street
b) The success of the play
c) The size of the theatre

Correct answers: 1a, 2c, 3a, 4c, 5c, 6b, 7c, 8b, 9c, 10a

Iconic view from New Jersey over Lower Manhattan with One World Trade Center

❻ Where do lots of wealthy New Yorkers escape to during the hot summer months?
a) Canada
b) The Hamptons
c) Bermuda

❼ What marks the northern end of Downtown?
a) The tip of Manhattan island
b) The south end of Central Park
c) 14th Street

❽ Where was hip hop invented?
a) Manhattan
b) The Bronx
c) Queens

❾ What can you do at the Bronx Riviera, on Coney Island and at Brighton Beach, which seems unusual for the city?
a) Ice skate
b) Not much, as there isn't a lot there
c) Lie on the beach and swim

❿ The High Line is a famous park today but what was it before?
a) Raised railway tracks
b) A motorway
c) Part of the port

INDEX

WE WANT TO HEAR FROM YOU!

Did you have a great holiday? Is there something on your mind? Whatever it is, let us know! Whether you want to praise the guide, alert us to errors or give us a personal tip – MARCO POLO would be pleased to hear from you. Please contact us by email:

sales@heartwoodpublishing.co.uk

We do everything we can to provide the very latest information for your trip. Nevertheless, despite all of our authors' thorough research, errors can creep in. MARCO POLO does not accept any liability for this.

PICTURE CREDITS
Cover photo: iStock/batuhanozdel
Photos: Horsten/Zeltner (171); huber-images: M. Borchi (22, 40), L. Caccarella (55), P. Canali (14/15 (©Wright, Frank Lyoyd), 26/27), F. Carovillano (48/49, 91), C. Cassaro (120/121, 168/169), C. Claudio (143), O. Fantuz (32, 44), Jockschat (12/13), S. Kremer (6/7, 47, 132/133, 138, 158/159, 162), C. Piccoli (58), M. Rellini (17, 42/43, 52, 56, 61, 94, 110/111, 124/125, 153), R. Taylor (25, 67), S. Torrione (116/117); Laif: Heeb (8, 102/103), F. Heuer (139), Linkel (86/87), Sasse (4, 35, 118); mauritius images: S. Pearce (145), Raga (98); mauritius images/age fotostock: R. Levine (93), J. Long (36), A. Patino (126/127); mauritius images/Alamy (38, 57, 73, 74, 78/79, 107), S. Foyt (65); mauritius images/Alamy/Alamy Stock Photos: D. Grandi (9); mauritius images/John Warburton-Lee: M. Falzone (149); mauritius images/Tetra Images (128/129); Schapowalow Images: A. Armellin (21), J. Banks (66), M. Borchi (68/69), O. Fantuz (50), A. Piai (166/167), M. Rellini (2/3, 154/155), R. Spila (outer front flap, inner front flap, 1), S. Torrione (63), Schapowalow Images/Lumiere/eStock Photo (77, 81, 100, 108, 115, 122, 152); Schapowalow/eStock Photo: C. Uriops (82/83, 84); Schapowalow/SIME: P. Canali (11), M. Rellini (112/113), M. Rellini (157); Schapowalow/Sime/eStock Photo: J. Foulkes (97), S. Torrione (130/131); G. Simeone (10); EQRoy/Shutterstock.com (161), Brian Logan Photgraphy/Shutterstock.com (164)

5th Edition – fully revised and updated 2023
Worldwide Distribution: Heartwood Publishing Ltd, Bath, United Kingdom
www.heartwoodpublishing.co.uk

Authors: Christina Horsten, Felix Zeltner
Editor: Jens Bey
Picture editor: Gabriele Forst
Cartography: © MAIRDUMONT, Ostfildern (pp. 134–135, 137, 141, 146–147, 148, 151, inner flap, outer flap, pull-out map); ©MAIRDUMONT, Ostfildern, using data from OpenStreetMap, Licence CC-BY-SA 2.0 (pp. 28–29, 31, 37, 41, 45, 53, 59, 70–71, 88–89, 104–105).
Cover design and pull-out map cover design: bilekjaeger_Kreativagentur with Zukunftswerkstatt, Stuttgart
Page design: Lucia Rojas

Heartwood Publishing credits:
Translated from the German by John Owen, Sophie Blacksell Jones, John Sykes, Jennifer Walcoff Neuheiser and Lindsay Chalmers-Gerbracht
Editors: Felicity Laughton, Kate Michell, Sophie Blacksell Jones, Rosamund Sales
Prepress: Summerlane Books, Bath
Printed in India

All rights reserved. No part of this book may be reproduced, stored in a retrieval system or transmitted in any form or by any means (electronic, mechanical, photocopying, recording or otherwise) without prior written permission from the publisher.or by any means (electronic, mechanical, photocopying, recording or otherwise) without prior written permission from the publisher.

MARCO POLO AUTHORS

CHRISTINA HORSTEN & FELIX ZELTNER are journalists who have lived in New York since 2012 with their two daughters. They enjoy moving house – one year they moved 14 times – and they have lived in all five boroughs of this giant conurbation. The constant upheaval and resettlement was the subject of their first book, which has attracted international attention and is the inspiration for lots of tips in this guide. *instagram.com/nyc12x12*

DOS & DON'TS

DON'T TAKE THE SLOW TRAINS!
Taking the subway across the city? Your journey will take considerably longer if you take a "local" train, so look out for "express" services whenever you can (but don't forget they don't stop everywhere).

DO ALWAYS BRING ID
Lots of sights require ID for security purposes, and most bars require proof of age even if you are clearly over 21, so always take a passport or driving licence out with you.

DO TAKE THE RIGHT TAXI
In Manhattan (up to 125th Street) the taxis are yellow; north of there and in the rest of the city they are green. Licensed city taxis and those from apps like Uber, Lift, Juno and Via are safe, so don't be seduced by offers from non-licensed taxis, even if they seem a great deal.

DON'T BE STINGY WITH YOUR TIPS
Americans often say you should "tip like Frank Sinatra" by which they mean "very generously". Tips – and here we don't mean "pieces of advice" – are part of life in America!

DON'T GIVE IN TO JET LAG
If you arrive in the afternoon, quickly freshen up and then go straight out into the city. And if you wake up way too early? Don't worry, the diners are open 24 hours a day for breakfast.